R.N. ELLIOTT'S MARKET LETTERS

1938-1946

RALPH NELSON ELLIOTT
Edited and foreworded by

Robert R. Prechter

Published by
New Classics Library

R.N. Elliott's Market Letters 1938-1946

Second Edition 2017
Second Printing 2018

Printed in the United States of America

ISBN: 978-1-61604-080-2
Library of Congress Control Number 2017937427

Publisher: New Classics Library
Gainesville, Georgia USA

Elliott Wave International
www.elliottwave.com
Address for comments: customercare@elliottwave.com

Acknowledgments

The main source for this material was the Library of Congress, to which Elliott sent copies of most of his periodicals. Some additions to that body of material were made by several friends, most notably John Hill of Commodities Research Institute.

The massive typing job was undertaken by Karen Latvala. Paula Roberson carefully arranged the book for printing and Dave Allman and Leigh Tipton prepared the charts for photographing.

Note

The publisher would like to obtain copies of missing material, including Educational Bulletins D through M, Educational Bulletin R, the bulletins entitled "Investment Timing" (late 1939) and "The Current Situation in the Stock Market" (April 1, 1940), Forecast Letters labeled "Confidential," and any other such material. A check of your elderly relatives' files and attics might prove rewarding.

This book is dedicated to that brilliant analyst and generous man, Charles J. Collins, without whose interest and assistance the great discoveries of R.N. Elliott may never have been published.

CONTENTS

FOREWORD

For years I have planned this book, and am very proud finally to present this compilation of treatises that have been out of print for five decades. Ralph Nelson Elliott (1871 - 1948) began forecasting the stock market at the age of 68 while suffering from a debilitating case of anemia contracted in South America. Despite a remarkably late start and difficult circumstances, he left a mark on the investment world that only a handful of giants have done.

The value of this material is substantial. First, Elliott's market letters contain a number of observations that are not found in his two books or his series of articles for *Financial World* magazine.[1] Second, several of his "real time" analyses are particularly insightful and original, expanding our knowledge of his unique genius. His fallible side also shows, as he misses several turns, sometimes in misapplying his own rules (particularly in the earlier issues, when he was just getting used to the saddle), sometimes rationalizing the reasons. Finally, these letters allow us to observe Elliott's progress in continuing to refine his observations of the Wave Principle as market events unfolded over a period of eight years (coinciding almost exactly with World War II).

Beginning in November 1938, shortly after the publication of his first monograph, "The Wave Principle," on August 31 of that year, Elliott began publishing at least two types of market commentary. The Interpretive Service consisted of explanatory market letters of two to four pages with charts. It sold for $60 per year. The Forecasting Service, sold for "conventional fees," provided one page market timing bulletins labeled "Confidential," of which very few survive. He also listed, without mentioning a price, "special reports for business executives," although no surviving papers are so labeled. It is possible that the otherwise unmarked treatise dated December 13, 1943 included in this volume was one of these reports.

Following the publication of his *Financial World* articles in the summer of 1939, Elliott began producing follow-up treatises that quickly evolved into a new Educational Service. He referred to the former as "circulars" and the labeled service issues variously as "letters" and "bulletins." From January 1940 on, he advertised only two services, the Educational Service, which he offered for $60 per year, and the Investment Forecast Service (referenced also as the Forecast service). Subscribers to the latter apparently then received both the Interpretive Letters and the Forecast Letters for $200 per year. After the publication of his second monograph, "Nature's Law," in 1946, which he considered his final educational statement on the Wave Principle, he ceased to offer the Educational Service and returned to advertising the Interpretive Service and the Forecast Service separately. It is a substantial consolation that, although the Educational Bulletins D through M, and R, are unavailable for this book, the majority of their substance is in "Nature's Law" (see Elliott's personal correspondence at the end of the Educational Bulletins section).

Elliott published his Interpretive and Forecast Letters at irregular intervals, aiming to issue them "on completion of a wave." His letters indeed were often issued at market turning points. In wave labeling fashion, Elliott notated his Interpretive Letters, the first service to be published, with numbers, and his Educational Bulletins with letters.

So few Forecast Letters survive that their number is indeterminate. Otherwise, Elliott wrote for 8 years, averaged 5 Interpretive Letters per year, published a total of 34 Interpretive Letters, and (based on available records) produced a total of 34 Educational Bulletins and circulars, an interesting, if coincidental, set of numbers produced by a student of the Fibonacci sequence.[2]

The price for Elliott's first treatise, "The Wave Principle," varied. As the book's freshness wore off and the bear market of the early 1940s wore on, it was lowered in price from $15 to $7.50 to $3. After the publication in June 1946 of "Nature's Law," which he offered for only $5, the price for his combined Interpretive Letters and Forecast Service was similarly lowered from $200 to $155 annually, probably in contemplation of producing fewer issues. In fact, only one post-"Nature's Law" page survives.

Although Elliott's market services ran concurrently, the presentation in this volume separates Interpretive and Forecast Letters from the Educational Bulletins and circulars. The reader will notice that while most of the Educational Bulletins stand alone as commentary on the Wave Principle, they occasionally contain references to market behavior and even to specific Interpretive Letters. In one or two instances, Elliott introduced new interpretive concepts in the Educational Bulletins that clearly would not have been employed in the Interpretive Letters published prior to those dates. Keep this chronology in mind as you read the earlier Interpretive Letters. For those readers who are not yet well versed in the basics of the Wave Principle, a capsule explanation entitled "The Basis of the Wave Principle" appears at the beginning of the Educational Bulletins section. I am certain that you will enjoy being a "subscriber" to R. N. Elliott's services and reading his observations on market behavior, made as he watched the patterns unfold.

—Robert R. Prechter, editor

THE ART OF FORECASTING

The behavior of cycles has been studied extensively by puzzled economists, bankers and business men. In this connection, the conservative *London Economist* in a recent issue said, in commenting upon the results of a long study of trade cycles made by Sir William Beveridge, the noted British economist:

> "Sir William's researches have emphasized once again that the more the trade cycle is studied, the more it seems to follow the pressure of forces which, if they are not wholly beyond the reach of human control, have at least enough of the inexorable in their nature to make the policies of governments resemble the struggles of fish caught in the tides. Sir William pointed out that the trade cycle ignores politics; he might have added that it overrides economic policies."

In an independent study of the available data, extending over a period of many years, the writer has observed certain recurring behavior of change in movement. Apparently these changes follow a natural law that inevitably influences the mass. Understanding of this law enables the close student to forecast the terminations of cycles by means of the market itself. The forecasting principle involved goes far beyond the concept of any known formula. This Principle forecasts and at the same time measures the extent, corrections and reversals of the various trends and cycles long before any supporting statistical evidence is available. A feature of unusual merit is the fact that the experienced student knows at all times the current position of the market in each cycle and therefore is forewarned of the approach of reversals.

The particulars of this forecasting Principle are disclosed and proved in a copyrighted treatise entitled:

THE WAVE PRINCIPLE

Price $15.00

In due course Interpretive Letters, based on the current market, will be available.

R. N. Elliott,
Discoverer

New York, N.Y.
25 Broad St.,

Hanover 2, 7887

FOOTNOTES

[1] All of Elliott's monographs and articles have been reprinted, along with an extensive biography, in *R.N. Elliott's Masterworks* (New Classics Library, 1980).

[2] He would have no doubt enjoyed the fact that *R.N. Elliott's Masterworks* was published 34 years after "Nature's Law" and this book 55 years after "The Wave Principle," neither by conscious design. Indeed, 8 years separated Elliott's two books and 13 years separate these two.

SERVICES: Description and Fees.

Two Services are available – Forecast and Interpretive.[1]

The Forecast Service is in the form of definite recommendations issued when developments indicate. These Letters are captioned "Confidential." They are brief, positive and devoid of tedious discussion of irrelevant events, statistics, politics, etc. This service fulfills two purposes:

(a) For students who wish to take advantage of my current recommendations but have not yet acquired sufficient proficiency to act on their own initiative.

(b) For those who are too busy with their own affairs to study "The Wave Principle."

The Interpretive Service consists of surveys in which recent market movements are charted and their waves classified and numbered. These Interpretive Letters analyze the behavior of such waves in clear and precise terms in accordance with my copyrighted Treatise, "Nature's Law," and are therefore valuable, as reference, for all time. This service is unique and economical for the reason that its aim is to enable the subscriber to become independent of services for all time.

The Treatise is a text book and discloses the behavior of cycles as they have been and will be for all time. The number of waves is constant, although their length and speed is variable. The price of the Treatise, "Nature's Law," is $5.00.

Service fees for 12 months

Interpretive Service	$57.50
Forecast Service	97.50
Combination (Interpretive & Forecast)	152.50

In order to provide an opportunity to observe the practical application of "The Wave Principle" without commitment to an annual contract, trial subscriptions are available:

	4 months
Interpretive Service	$20.00
Forecast Service	$33.00
Combined Interpretive & Forecast	$51.00

If both services are taken on trial or by the year, a copy of the Treatise, "Nature's Law," will be furnished gratis.

R.N. Elliott

Date:

To R. N. Elliott,
63 Wall St., New York 5, N.Y.

I enclose my check. The amount indicates my wishes.

Please print: Name:

Address:

FOOTNOTES

[1] See Foreword.

THE WAVE PRINCIPLE

63 WALL STREET
NEW YORK 5, N.Y.

R. N. ELLIOTT

S E R V I C E S : Description and Fees.

Two Services are available, - Forecast and Interpretive.

The Forecast Service: Is in the form of definite recommendations issued when developments indicate. These Letters are captioned "Confidential". They are brief, positive and devoid of tedious discussion of irrelevant events, statistics, politics, etc. This Service fulfills two purposes:

(a) For students who wish to take advantage of my current recommendations but have not yet acquired sufficient proficiency to act on their own initiative.

(b) For those who are too busy with their own affairs to study "The Wave Principle".

The Interpretive Service: consists of surveys in which recent market movements are charted and their waves classified and numbered. These Interpretive Letters analyze the behavior of such waves in clear and precise terms in accordance with my copyrighted Treatise "Nature's Law" and are therefore valuable, as reference, for all time. This Service is unique and economical for the reason that its aim is to enable the subscriber to become independent of services for all time.

The Treatise is a text book and discloses the behavior of cycles as they have been and will be for all time. The number of waves is constant although their length and speed is variable. The price of the Treatise "Nature's Law" is $5.00.

	Service fees for 12 months
Interpretive Service,	$57.50
Forecast Service,	97.50
Combination (Interpretive and Forecast),	152.50

In order to provide an opportunity to observe the practical application of The Wave Principle without commitment to an annual contract, trial subscriptions are available to the

	4 Months
Interpretive Service	$20.00
Forecast Service	33.00
Combined Interpretive and Forecast	51.00

If both Services are taken on trial or by the year, a copy of the Treatise, "Nature's Law" will be furnished gratis.

R. N. Elliott.

- -

Date . . . .

To R. N. Elliott,
63 Wall St., New York 5, N. Y.

I enclose my check . The amount indicates my wishes.

Please print: Name . . . .

Address . . . .

. . . .

Interpretive Letters and Forecast Letters

R. N. ELLIOTT
25 BROAD ST.
NEW YORK

HAnover 2 7887

Nov. 10, 1938

THE WAVE PRINCIPLE

A new market service is herewith inaugurated under the title of:

Interpretative Letter No. 1.

This service is unique in that it will not forecast but apply The Wave Principle to the recent movement for the benefit of students of the Treatise on the subject.

The Treatise is a Text Book and students are expected to apply The Wave Principle to subsequent waves and practice forecasting under the guidance of the Treatise.

A cycle which began March 31st last has just completed its five waves. The first two are shown in the Treatise on page 49 but are included herein to furnish a complete picture of the cycle.

Hereafter Letters will be issued on completion of a wave and not await the entire cycle. In this manner students may learn how to do their own forecasting and at no expense. The phenomenon and its practical application become increasingly interesting because the market continually unfolds new examples to which may be applied unchanging rules.

No two movements are exactly alike, nevertheless the phenomenon of The Wave Principle invariably applies as described in the Treatise. Likewise the same analysis applies to cycles of whatever size. Compare the current cycle with those shown on pages 37, 38 and 42 of the Treatise.

Key to numbers and Letters at wave endings on charts shown in Letters:

	Designation	Where placed	Indication
1.	Roman numerals	Advancing movements	
2.	Ordinary numbers	Advancing movements	Next degree lower than Roman numerals
3.	Capital Letters	Corrections	
4.	Small letters	Both advances and corrections	Next degree lower than numbers and Capital Letters
5.	x	Preceding small letters, a to e, as for example "xa"	Extensions
6.	OT	Preceding an irregular type of correction	Orthodox Top
7.	# and *	Anywhere	"See note below"
8.	T	Anywhere	See Treatise, page & paragraf
9.	C	Anywhere	See chart No.

R. N. Elliott.

Treatise $15.00,
Interpretive Letters $60. per annum,
Forecasting Service, conventional fees,
Special reports for business executives.

THE WAVE PRINCIPLE[1]

A new market service is herewith[2] inaugurated under the title of:

INTERPRETIVE LETTER No. 1

March 31 to November 10, 1938

This service is unique in that it will not forecast but apply The Wave Principle to the recent movement for the benefit of students of the Treatise on the subject.

The Treatise is a text book, and students are expected to apply The Wave Principle to subsequent waves and practice forecasting under the guidance of the Treatise.

A cycle[3] which began March 31st last has just completed its five waves.[4] The first two are shown in the Treatise on page 49, but are included herein to furnish a complete picture of the cycle.

Hereafter, Letters will be issued on completion of a wave and not await the entire cycle. In this manner, students may learn how to do their own forecasting and at no expense. The phenomenon and its practical application become increasingly interesting because the market continually unfolds new examples to which may be applied unchanging rules.

No two movements are exactly alike. Nevertheless, the phenomenon of The Wave Principle invariably applies as described in the Treatise. Likewise the same analysis applies to cycles of whatever size. Compare the current cycle with those shown on pages 37, 38 and 42 of the Treatise.

Key to numbers and Letters at wave endings on charts shown in Letters:

Designation	Where Placed	Indication
1. Roman numerals	Advancing movements	
2. Ordinary numbers	Advancing movements	Next degree lower than Roman numerals
3. Capital Letters	Corrections	
4. Small letters	Both advances[5] and corrections	Next degree lower than numbers and capital letters
5. x	Preceding small letters, a to 3, as for example "xa"	Extensions
6. OT	Preceding an irregular type of correction	Orthodox Top
7. # and *	Anywhere	"See note below"
8. T	Anywhere	"See Treatise," page and paragraph
9. C	Anywhere	See chart No.

Treatise $15.00,
Interpretive Letters $60 per annum
Forecasting Service, conventional fees,
Special reports for business executives.

Below is an outline of the March-November cycle showing the main waves, and channel (dashed lines) as applied when wave (III) extends, as in the present instance.[6] The parallel line furnishes an approximate idea as to where wave (V) may terminate.

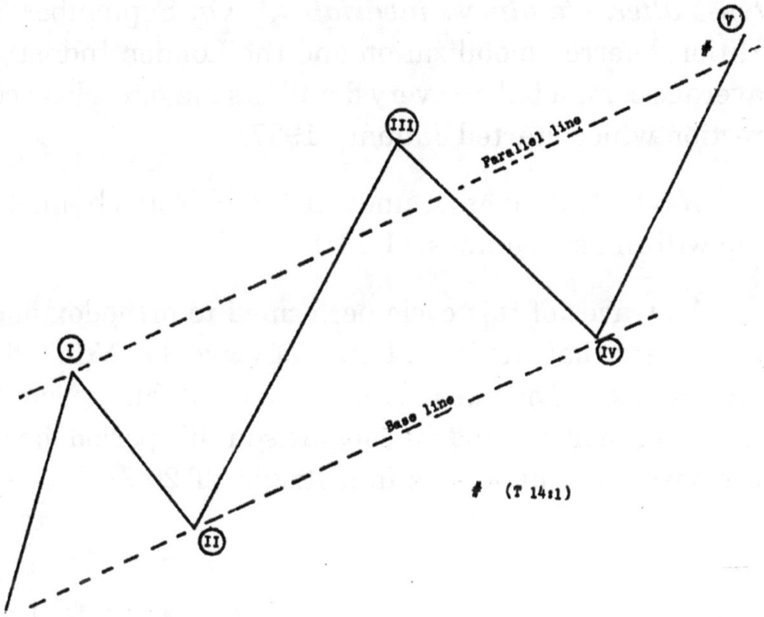

When the student masters The Wave Principle, he may apply it to any human activity, averages, groups, individual stocks, bonds, commodities, production, life insurance, gasoline consumption or whatnot. (T 3:2 also 31 to 36).[7]

Wave (I), 24 points, *5 waves, which confirms 97.46 as the bottom because it is the first upward 5 wave movement of this degree since March 1937.*

Wave (II), (first correction), *"flat" type, which calls for zigzag type in the second correction (wave (IV)).* Wave C is composed of 5 waves, a to e as per rule. (T 16:3).[8]

Wave Ⓘ̅Ⓘ̅, 40 points, extended.[9] Volume and speed were unusually high due to reversal of volume cycle June 18/20. (T 25, 35 & 50).

Wave Ⓘ̅Ⓥ, 19 points, zigzag type.[10] *Zigzag and flat types alternate almost invariably.*[11] On September 28, Hitler deferred mobilization and the London Industrial average completed, in every detail, its major cyclical correction which started January 1937.

Wave Ⓥ, 31 points, unextended.[12] Note channel at top within dashed lines. (T 14:1).

All waves of this cycle performed in orthodox manner except that the last Minute of wave 3 of V failed to materialize.[13] The Rail average completed this movement in proper manner, and for comparison this period for the Rails is shown under the Industrials. (T 20:2)

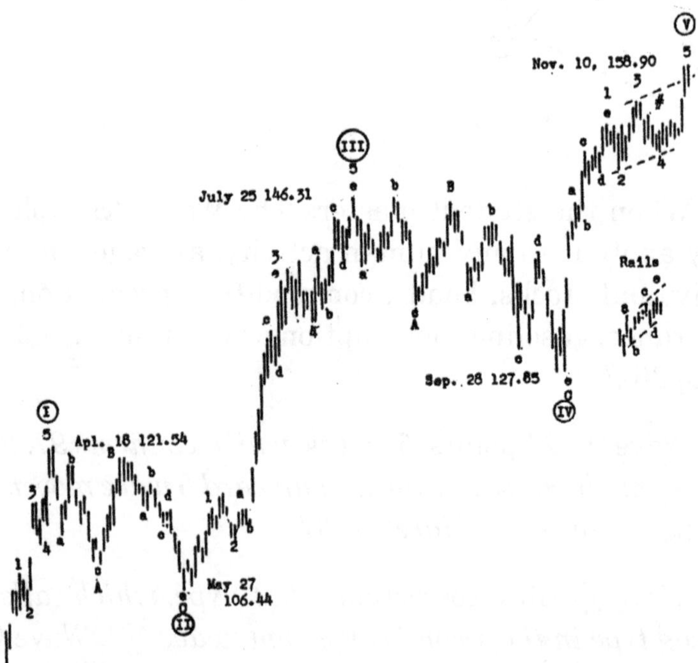

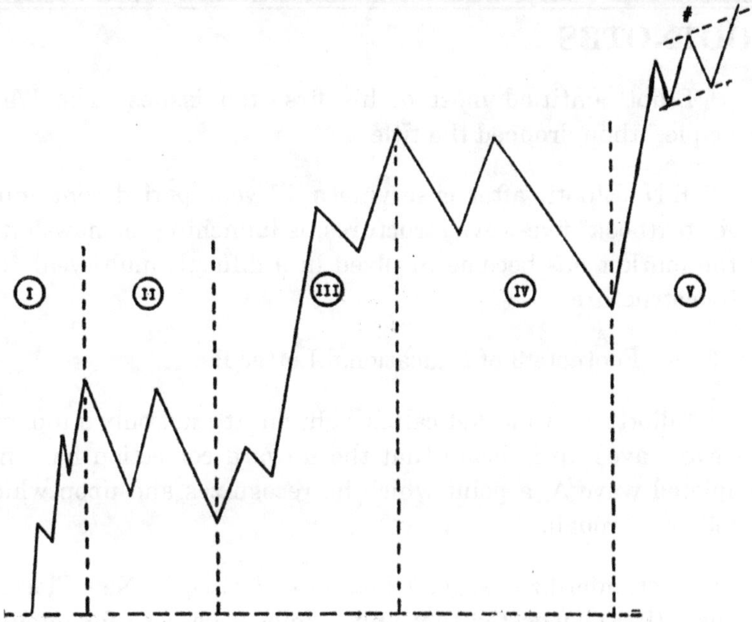

All five waves of this cycle except wave Ⓘ were subdivided into three degrees. This chart is repeated above, but with the lowest degree of waves omitted.

In the previous chart, all three degrees of waves are shown, but on the above chart, the lowest degree waves have been omitted. Also, vertical dashed lines separate the main waves. The purpose is to simplify for new students of the Wave Principle.

In this cycle, as in all other of whatever degree, the subdivisions are invariably five for advances and three for corrections, that is, every cycle has 21 waves of the next lower degree.

#Note the channel (dashed lines) and "throw-over" at the extreme top of Ⓥ. (T 14:1).

R.N. Elliott

FOOTNOTES

[1] Elliott entitled most of his first ten issues "The Wave Principle," then dropped the title.

2 R.N. Elliott, after observing a 17 year period containing large "textbook" five-wave structures, is launching his newsletter as the market has become involved in a difficult multi-year corrective structure.

3 See Footnote 3 of Educational Letter B.

[4] Elliott's first market call is right on. It's not only a top, but the five waves up indicate that the upward correction has only completed wave A, a point which he recognizes and upon which he follows through.

[5] To standardize usage, *Elliott Wave Principle* (New Classics Library, 1978) suggested that only numbers be used for impulse waves, letters for corrections.

[6] Frost and I offered as good practice the exact same idea for the upper parallel line independently in *Elliott Wave Principle* (see pages 64 and 153) prior to having read Elliott's market letters.

[7] Elliott made references to page numbers in his textbook, in the same manner as *The Elliott Wave Theorist* references *Elliott Wave Principle.*

[8] Wave c (the third wave of C) is the shortest, breaking one of Elliott's later rules, postulated in "Nature's Law."

[9] Wave c of 3 of (III) evidenced the greatest acceleration, the typical occurrence as discussed in *Elliott Wave Principle.*

[10] Elliott counts three waves in wave A, but calls it a zigzag correction, contrary to his own description.

[11] Waves (II) and (IV) are similar, and it is not clear that Alternation occurred.

[12] Elliott's counts within this wave contains a large overlap of waves 1 and 4, which Elliott later disallowed in "Nature's Law." Based on the wave labelings in his Interpretive Letters, it is unlikely that he drew the non-overlap conclusion prior to 1945. A better wave count is shown below.

[13] The count above eliminates this apparent problem.

INTERPRETIVE LETTER No. 2

March 31 to November 28, 1938

Interpretive Letter No. 1 covered the period from March 31 to November 10, 1938, during which a complete cycle developed. Three different designs were shown to assist the student in the application of The Wave Principle, which is the object of these Letters. On the next page of the present Letter, the same period is shown employing the weekly range instead of the daily range. The correction of the cycle referred to is also shown, not only in the weekly range, but separately, in the daily range.

On the weekly range chart, all waves of the cycle are clear except those of wave Ⓘ, the subdivisions of which are clear in the daily range in Letter No. 1.

In fast markets the daily range is essential, and the hourly useful, if not always essential. On the contrary, when the daily range becomes obscure due to slow speed and long duration of waves, condensation into weekly range clarifies. (T 26:9:10 and 27:3).[1]

From the extreme top, November 10, downward to November 28 is the correction to the cycle. This is shown both in the weekly range and daily range, the latter in a small chart below. The smaller chart is double the scale of that used in the weekly range chart. *The first downward wave* Ⓐ[2] *is clearly subdivided into five lesser waves, which indicates that the correction will be of the zigzag type. (T 17:1 A). If the first downward wave had been composed of three small waves, the correction would have been of the "flat" type. Wave* Ⓑ *is composed of the usual 3 smaller waves, which constitute the correction or hesitation of the downward movement.*

Wave Ⓒ, the second downward wave, companion to Ⓐ, would normally have been composed of 5 smaller waves, as was Ⓐ, but there is only one wave, six points. Incidentally, it is important to note that wave Ⓒ is composed of 5 very small waves, i.e., of the degree next lower than those which composed Ⓐ. These waves are visible only in the hourly, particularly in the Dow Jones 65 Composite.

Nevertheless, wave Ⓒ is incomplete, technically. Incomplete waves are neither common nor rare. "Unusual" is perhaps the proper term. Two examples are found in waves 3 and 4 of the large triangle which occurred between October 1937 and February 1938 (T 47 and 48). For convenient reference, they are shown below.

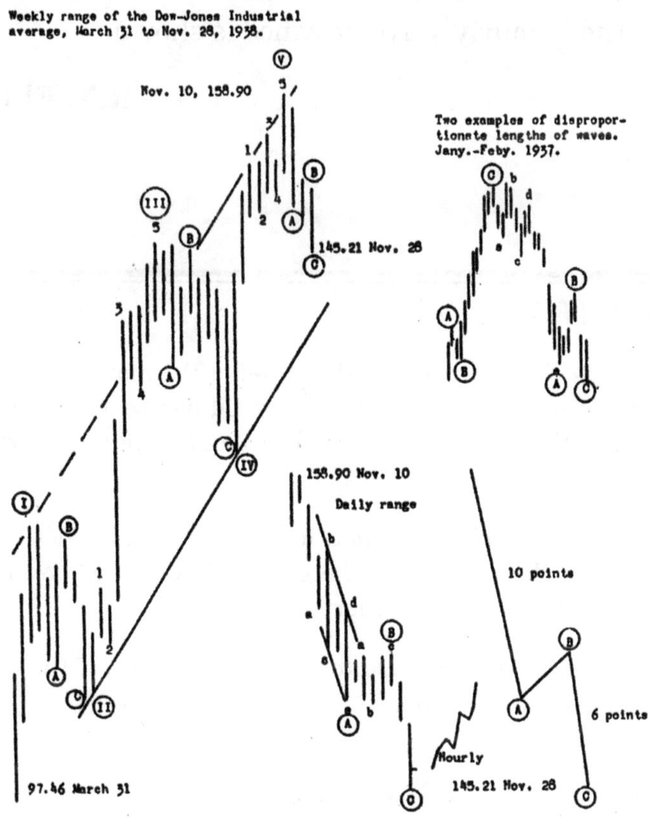

Normally, with the assistance of The Wave Principle, buying may be exercised during the last wave downward, but here is an unusual case when that cannot be done for obvious reasons. Proof that the abbreviated[3] wave Ⓒ had ended lies in the fact that, following the low point at 145.21, a reversal occurred which was composed of 5 waves (hourly). Five waves upward has no place here if the decline is to continue. Therefore wave Ⓒ has terminated, and subsequent to the 5 hourly waves, a correction of 3 waves, also hourly, should follow, which will be confirmatory evidence that reversal of trend has occurred. The first paragraph on page 3 of Letter No. 1 reads:

> "Wave Ⓘ, 5 waves, confirms 97.46 as bottom because *it is the first upward wave movement of this degree since March 1937.*"

On the previous page, near the small chart at the bottom, the 5 hourly-wave advance is shown.

R.N. Elliott

FOOTNOTES

[1] Elliott's observation that the speed of the move should determine the scale upon which it is observed has been overlooked by Elliott practitioners. It's an interesting and perhaps important point.

[2] In the original letter, Elliott used parentheses to designate these waves in the text, while the charts show circles. We have made the text conform to the charts.

[3] I.e., abbreviated relative to the nearest wave of the same degree in the same direction.

INTERPRETIVE LETTER No. 3

November 10 to December 24, 1938

A market letter that is purely educational and not a forecasting service is novel and the distinction has not been generally understood. While the phenomenon of The Wave Principle is a recent disclosure, it has always existed in all human activities; therefore, history is replete with ample evidence and the Treatise portrays a generous supply. Attention is invited to the usual announcement that the Interpretive Letter Service is $60 per annum, whereas Forecasting advice is furnished at conventional fees.

Below is shown the correction from the top of November 10, and the first upward wave of the current cycle. Attention is now invited to the forecasting implications of the correction, which were intentionally omitted in Letter No. 2.

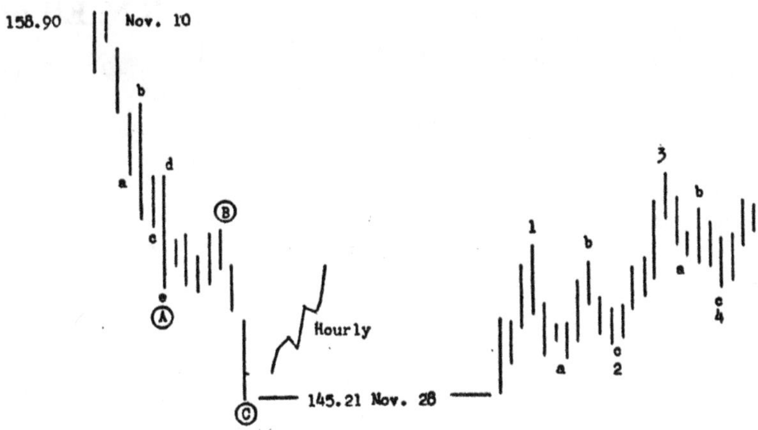

Compare the correction detailed above with the zigzag pattern in the Treatise on page 17, paragraph 1. (This and the other two patterns are complete corrections). *The first*

movement of the zigzag, wave Ⓐ, in both the Treatise and that detailed below, is composed of five small waves, which is the cue to observe. Five waves downward in Ⓐ, whether daily or hourly, forecast two things:

A. that the correction will be zigzag, as shown, and
B. that it will constitute the entire correction.[1]

I expected that wave Ⓒ would be composed of five smaller waves, the same as Ⓐ. Instead, however, an abbreviated wave appeared, which occurs occasionally. *The hourly pattern of five waves upward from the close of November 28 announced two things*:

A. the end of wave Ⓒ and complete correction, therefore
B. reversal of trend.

Interpretive Letter No. 4 will be unusually interesting, as the first advance from 145.21 of November 28 presents a coincidence never before noted.

R.N. Elliott

FOOTNOTES

[1] Elliott later allowed for the "double zigzag" formation.

INTERPRETIVE LETTER No. 4

November 10, 1938 to January 13, 1939

On the next page are shown four charts designated by the last four letters of the alphabet in double circles.[1]

W In Letter No. 3, I referred to a novel coincidence. Between November 10 and December 28, 1938, the D J Industrial Average made a fairly good triangle pattern. A triangle should have five waves, each of which should be composed of not more than 3 waves, which is complied with in this instance, although there is some doubt as to waves 4 and 5. The implication of the *apparent* triangle was upward from the apex at (5) and therefore in harmony with the bullish indications described in Letter No. 3. For numerous reasons it appeared doubtful that the pattern was a real triangle, and this has been confirmed. If the triangle were legitimate, it would have been a complete correction to the previous cycle, which was not the case as *the apex has since been violated.*

X This chart shows the D-J Industrial Average from November 10, 1938 at 158.90 to January 13, 1939 at 146.03. The implications of the correction from November 10 to 28, as described in Letter No. 3, were fulfilled with the exception that the 5th Minor wave between "d" and "e" (see dashed line) failed to materialize.[2] Such failures are exceedingly rare and their importance is gauged by the degree of the wave in question, which in this case is minor. When such failures occur, there is usually an *effort* to fulfill, which was absent in this instance. (Treatise 20:2). One minor failure occurred in the March-November, 1938 cycle, October 25th, as described in Letter No. 1. At that time, certain other Industrial averages and the

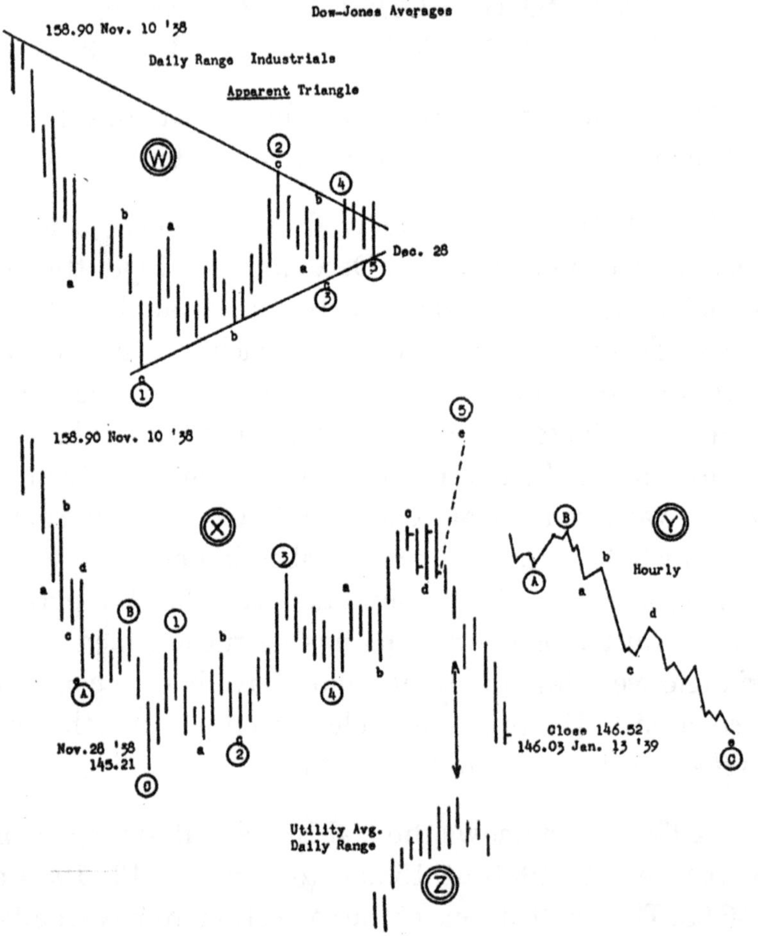

D-J Rails did not participate in the failure. In the present instance, the rails participated but the Utilities did not. See chart **Z**.

> Interpretive Letter No. 3 says:
> "I expected that wave Ⓒ would be composed of 5 smaller waves, the same as Ⓐ. Instead, however, an abbreviated wave appeared."

It may be that incompletion of wave Ⓒ at 145.21 on November 28 caused a failure of the 5th Minor mentioned in the previous paragraph. I do not recall a similar incompletion. *Experience indicates that incomplete corrections are bullish.* Wave C was short some 4 points of its planned objective. The subsequent advance should have had about 4 points more and completed 5 waves.

In my forecasting service, I have frequently warned subscribers that in the current position of the Grand Super Cycle, movements may be sensitive to current news and therefore erratic in many ways, such as, for example, the failure described.

One of the many advantages of The Wave Principle is that it discloses irregularities. Without The Wave Principle, there are just two movements, "up" and "down". The Wave Principle is not a "method" nor a "theory," but simply the behavior of a phenomenon.

Y The chart at the extreme right is the hourly record from the orthodox top of December 30 at 154.94 (c), to the bottom at 146.03 January 13, 1939. Note that this correction is composed of 3 waves, Ⓐ, Ⓑ & Ⓒ. Ⓐ and Ⓑ are composed of 3 waves each, and Ⓒ of 5 waves, as customary.

When volume is very low, the inactivity of certain high priced stocks in the Dow Jones Industrial Average causes abnormalities in the smallest hourly waves. Such stocks as Allied Chemical, International Business Machines, Eastman Kodak, etc. may not appear on the tape for several hours, and if the market has moved considerably between sales of these stocks, the effect can easily be visualized.

R.N. Elliott

FOOTNOTES

[1] Elliott's chart designations use variously circles, double circles, parentheses and quotation marks. For simplicity, single bold faced letters are used for the chart references in the text of this book, while the original designations on the charts have been left intact.

[2] Actually, the price bar following d did make a new high, which is enough for e, but not enough to carry the market above the 1938 high. I have found reasoning such as "waves failing to materialize" a detriment to the proper application of the Wave Principle. Elliott later described formations which took into account the reality of the market's behavior, and thus eliminated the necessity for such comments. In fact, the lack of a clear five waves up apparently had a bearish message, the consequences of which Elliott then had to deal with in Interpretive Letter No. 5.

INTERPRETIVE LETTER No. 5

November 10, 1938 to January 26, 1939

Charts below are designated by the letters **V**, **W**, **X**, **Y**, and **Z** in double circles.

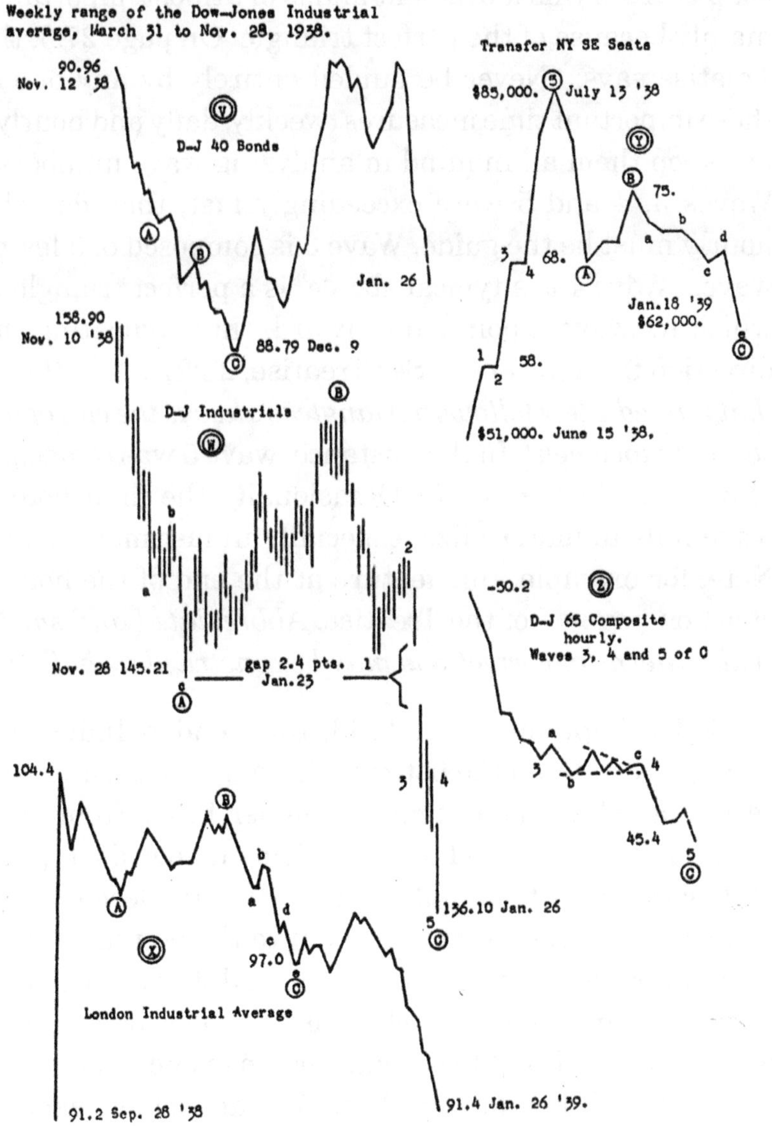

W The extent of the decline of the D-J Industrial Average requires a new analysis as shown by letters and numbers. The most important feature is the period covered by waves 3, 4 and 5 of ©.

Z The D-J Composite 65 hourly furnishes the clearest picture of this movement and is of utmost importance mainly because of the perfect triangle. On page 27:3, the Treatise says: "Never be guided entirely by any one of these important time measures (weekly, daily and hourly), but keep them all in mind in analyzing wave numbers." Waves 3, 4 and 5 were exceedingly fast, therefore the hourly must be the guide. Wave 3 is composed of 5 lesser waves. Wave 4 is a typical abc. "c" is a perfect triangle of which its wave 2 points downward, thus indicating the direction from the apex. (See Treatise, 22:2 A.) *The thrust that immediately follows a triangle is always the end of the current movement*. In this instance, wave 5 was composed of 3 waves instead of 5.[1] Occasionally the final hourly wave fails to materialize, especially in fast movements. Note, for example, this feature at the end of the hourly chart on page 47 of the Treatise. *Abbreviated and shriveled patterns of corrections may be construed as bullish.*

X On September 28, 1938, the London Industrial average registered the bottom of a complete cyclical correction at 91.2 which began December 1936. From 91.2, a bull pattern occurred to 104.4. Then followed a typical ABC correction terminating at © (97.0), December 9, 1938. (See chart). From that point to the bottom at 91.4 on January 26, an irregularity occurred that has no precedent insofar as my researches disclose. This irregularity was a distinct threat to our market when one remembers that although London and New York are seldom exactly in gear with each other, both make important reversals simultaneously, or nearly so. This irregularity carried the London market within a fraction of a new bear market low and could have added confusion here.

Y Correction of our volume cycle also contributed to weakness in our market, and is still present. The cycle of transfers of Stock Exchange (SE) seats harmonizes with the money value of stock transactions on the NYSE. This is shown in the charts on pages 35 and 36 of the Treatise and discussed on pages 24:6:7, 25 and 31:4. Chart **Y** shows the movement from the bottom at $51,000 on June 15, 1938, to date, which includes a bull swing to July 13, 1938, and then to present writing a normal ABC correction to $62,000. Some further sale may be made in the nature of a forced transaction, in which case a figure slightly lower than 62 might register without changing the indications of the patterns. This graph indicates that we may expect an increase in volume shortly.

Letters Nos. 3 and 4 describe the first decline from the November top at 158.90 to 145.21 as a zigzag and therefore the end of the correction, although it was an abbreviated pattern. During the same period, the D-J bond average **V** declined in zigzag pattern but completed the design shown in Treatise 17:1A, and has not violated the bottom then made. The Utility average has not violated the bottom made December 9, and on the contrary has progressed materially in the second cycle. The Rails violated their December bottom by only one point.

It is therefore evident that severe pressure was exerted on European holders of American industrial leaders, causing them to involuntarily dump wholesale on our thin market January 23rd, thus creating a gap of 2.4 pts. in our Industrial average.[2]

R.N. Elliott

FOOTNOTES

[1] Elliott labels wave c of 4 a triangle, going against his rule that "c" waves are always "fives." If he had started his triangle at the bottom of wave 3, allowing wave b of the triangle to make a new low and labeled the next three movements waves c, d and e of 4, he would then have an excellent structure and the proper five waves in wave 5.

[2] This kind of talk is fundamentally anti-Wave Principle, and is clearly included to help rationalize a minor mistake. Still, this letter calls a short term low to the day.

INTERPRETIVE LETTER No. 6

January 26 to April 11, 1939

Charts below are designated by letters **W**, **X** and **Y** in double circles, all of which depict the Dow Jones Industrial Average.

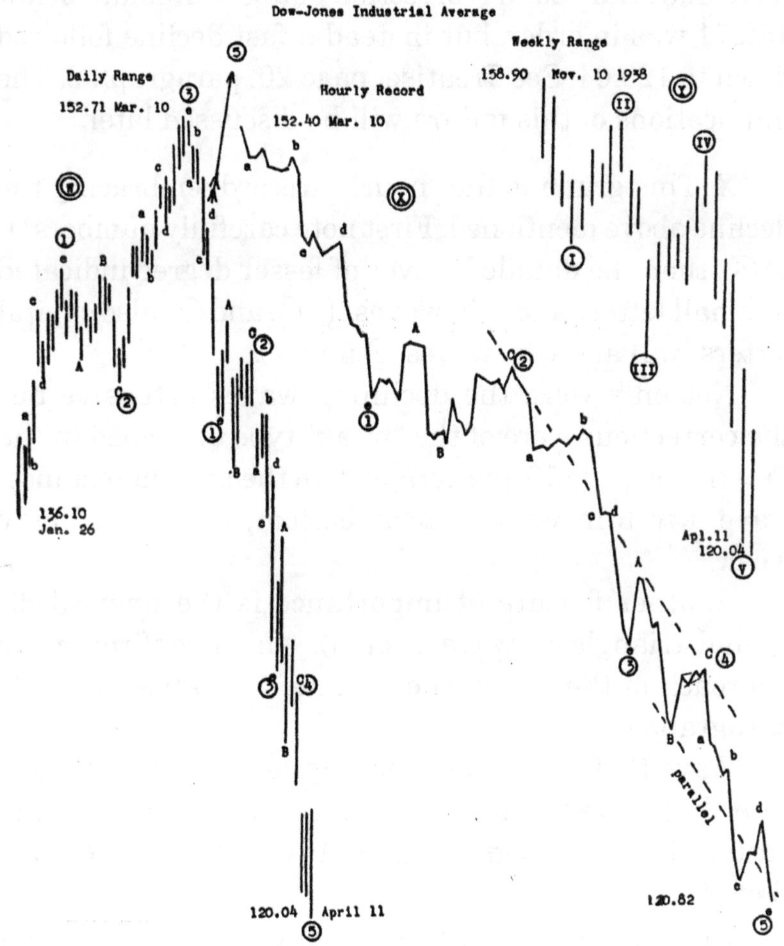

W is the Daily range from January 26 at 136.10 to April 11 at 120.04. It is a continuation of graph **W** Letter 5 which terminated at 136.10. Graph **W** herewith shows the advance above 136.10 in 3 waves to 152.71. Attention is invited to the arrow at the top pointing to "(5)" which indicates that another advancing wave, wave 5, should have materialized.[1] A correction of about 4 points below 152.71 was in order, but instead a fast decline followed down to 120.04. See Treatise, page 20, paragraph 2. The implications of this failure will be discussed later.

X This graph is the "hourly" record, embracing the decline above mentioned. First note carefully numbers ① to ⑤, then the detailed waves of lesser degree indicated by small letters a to e, in waves ①, ③ and ⑤, also capital letters A, B and C of waves ② and ④.

Not only were the declining waves extensive but the corrections were of the "weak" type described in the Treatise on page 19, paragraph 3. In the present instance, wave a to b in wave 5, near bottom, was exceedingly weak.

Another feature of importance is the upward diagonal triangle in wave C of ④, which confirms near approach of the end of the decline.[2] (Treatise page 21, paragraph 4.)

Wave B of ④ has 3 lesser degree waves which indicate that wave ④ had not finished. An example of this pattern is shown in graph, page 46 of Treatise (see wave B of (4)).

High and accelerating speed of the decline reflected the violence of European news, notwithstanding which The Wave Principle never failed.

Note the base line drawn from wave ② to wave ④ and its parallel. Also the "throw-over," which is described on page 14, paragraph 1 of the Treatise.

Y This graph is the weekly range from November 10, 1938 to April 11, 1939 and is a continuation of the chart of the same description in Letter No. 2. The end of Wave ⒾⅡ is 136.10 on January 26, the orthodox termination of the correction to the previous advancing cycle.[3] Wave Ⓘⅴ clearly shows 3 waves, whereas it should have had 5 waves, as explained under **W** of this Letter.[1]

R.N. Elliott

FOOTNOTES

[1] Clearly this is an a-b-c rally. The comments in Footnote 2 of Interpretive Letter No. 5 apply, and this time Elliott missed an important peak.

[2] Judging from the attendant graph and his reference to the bearish aspects of upward diagonal triangles in "The Wave Principle," Elliott probably meant to say "near approach of the end of the *rally*."

[3] The orthodox end of a correction never occurs prior to its price low, according to Elliott's own description. He doesn't say this ever again.

INTERPRETIVE LETTER No. 7
March 31, 1938 to April 11, 1939

In Letter No. 6, paragraph **W**, I advised that "the implications of this failure will be discussed later."

On the next page will be found 6 graphs designated by letters **U**, **V**, **W**, **X**, **Y** and **Z**.

W This graph is copied from the Treatise, page 17, paragraph 1, zigzag pattern.

X Is the same pattern as **W** but enlarged in order to designate the application to the current bear market which started on March 1937, as shown at the top. The end of Wave A is indicated as March 1938. Wave B of graph **X** is enlarged and detailed in graph **Y**.

Y This graph embraces the period that the market has traveled from:

March 1938 to November 1938	(wave a)
November 1938 to January 26, 1939	(wave b)
January 26 to March 10, 1939	(wave c)

The end of the solid line corresponds to 152.71 on March 10 in graph **U**, and the dotted line covers a movement that failed to materialize.[1]

U This graph is the weekly range of the Dow Jones Industrials for the period covered by graph **Y**. The arrow pointing to "e" corresponds to the dotted line in graph (Y). The movement from 152.71 on March 10 to 120.04 on April 11 is the first wave below B of graph **X**.

So much for the position of the current market as it relates to patterns in the Treatise.

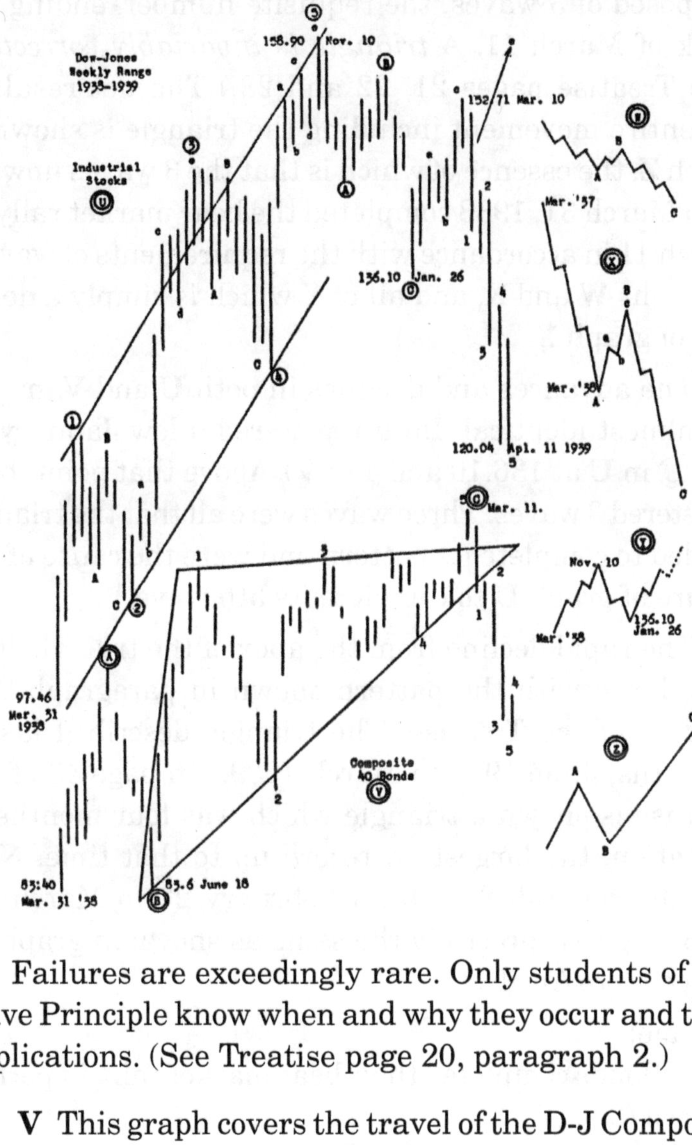

Failures are exceedingly rare. Only students of The Wave Principle know when and why they occur and their implications. (See Treatise page 20, paragraph 2.)

V This graph covers the travel of the D-J Composite Bonds average for identically the same period as graph U above it. This average elected to travel in a pattern decidedly different from the Industrial curve **U**. The first two waves, Ⓐ and Ⓑ, are the same type as waves 1 and 2 of **U**, but thereafter, wave Ⓒ, a triangle,[2] formed as per enclosure.[3] The 5th leg of the triangle (4 to 5) is composed of 3 waves, the requisite number, ending the week of March 11. *A triangle is invariably corrective.* (See Treatise pages 21, 22 and 23.) The net result of the entire movement including the triangle is shown in graph **Z**, the essence of which is that the 3 waves upward from March 31, 1938 completed the bear market rally on March 11 in accordance with the requirements of wave B of graphs **W** and **X**, and all of **Y** which is simply a detail of B of graph **X**.

The advances and declines in both **U** and **V** graphs are almost identical. Both registered a low January 26 (see © in **U** at 136.10 and 4 in **V**). Above that point, both registered 3 waves. Three waves were all that the triangle needed to complete its pattern and were the cause of the failure of graph **U** to complete its 5th wave.[4]

The rapid decline from the apex of the triangle is in accordance with the pattern shown in paragraph 2 A, page 22 of the Treatise. The triangle described lasted 9 months, June 1938 to March 1939. On page 48 of the Treatise is shown a triangle which was four months in formation, the largest on record up to that time. Note also the rapid decline from February 23 to March 31, 1938, page 47, precisely the same as shown in graph **U**, March 10 to April 11.

Resume:

1. Bonds completed their bear market rally in perfect pattern (3 legs),

2. Rail average and Rail Equipment group completed triangles similar to Bonds,

3. Utility average completed its rally in still another pattern, termed a "double 3,"

4. Industrial stocks (graph **U**) lacked only one relatively small wave to complete its rally.

R.N. Elliott

FOOTNOTES

[1] Although his ensuing discussion of the Composite 40 Bonds explains his reasoning, to claim that this wave c in the Dow failed to contain five waves *and* failed to go above the peak of wave a, and yet is wave c of B anyway is nonsense. Actually, the entire decline is wave B. Wave C occurs thereafter, in coming months.

[2] He obviously should call it a *diagonal* triangle.

[3] He means "as per the lines drawn on the chart."

[4] This statement contradicts Elliott's later more useful observation (possibly made as a result of this experience) that different markets behave, and should be interpreted, independently (see Footnote 5 of Interpretive Letter No. 11, Educational Bulletin C and Footnote 2 of Educational Bulletin B).

INTERPRETIVE LETTER No. 8

April 11 to June 9, 1939

Federal Securities: Graph **W** on the next page indicates that long term Government Bonds have completed a 7½ year bull cycle to be followed presently by a major decline. All classes of Government securities present the same picture.[1]

Triangles: As shown in graph **Z** on the next page, the Dow Jones Industrial Average completed a triangular outline on June 30, 1939 at 128.97 which began in March 1937. This is not an orthodox triangle as all legs are composed of 5 Minors instead of 3 (except the last which has 3). Moreover, it does not serve as a corrective, such as wave 2 or 4, because it originates at the top of a bull market and points downward. In connection therewith, note the following references in the Treatise:

	Page	*Paragraph*
Diagonal triangles	21	4
Horizontal triangles	21	2 & 3; note thrust from apex
Horizontal triangles	22	2A
Triangle Oct '37-Feb '38	47	
Triangle Oct '37-Feb '38	48	
Minor waves of triangles	23	5
Volume during triangles	24	4

A similar outline starting September 1929 is likewise unorthodox for reasons cited. These outlines are merely coincidences and are mentioned here because of numerous inquiries.[2]

Thrusts: From the apex of an orthodox triangle, such as those described in the Treatise on pages 47 and 48 and Letter No. 7, a rapid movement occurs in the direction of waves 2 and 4 of the triangle, and this I call a "thrust." When a thrust is completed, a rebound of some importance follows, such as occurred from March 31, 1938 and April 11, 1939. The extent of the rebound depends on other circumstances.

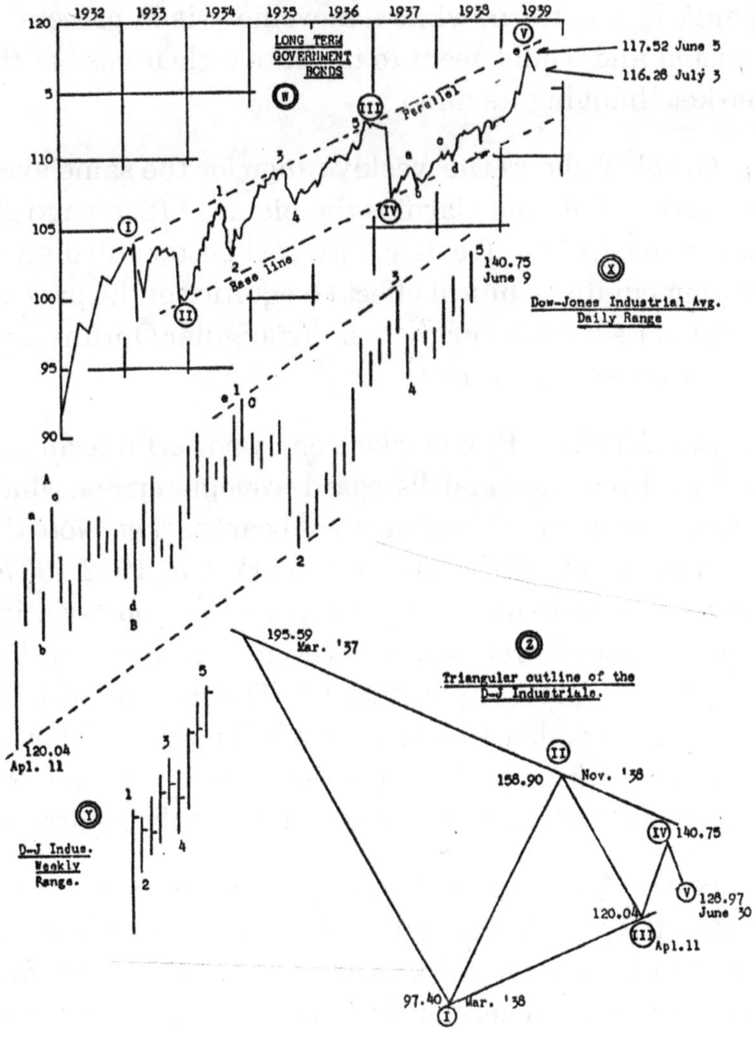

Graph **X** above shows the Dow Jones Industrial Average, daily range from April 11 to June 9, 1939. This movement started as a "flat," which would have been followed by a continuation of the decline. The letters A, B and C mark the waves of a "flat." A and C should have been about level, likewise B and the bottom. The small letters a to e mark the waves to correspond with an advance and thus form wave 1 of the next higher degree. Between c and d the market changed its mind. This change in a pattern, while a movement is in process, is unusual and would seem to indicate a clear case of the market changing its mind.[3]

Graph **Y** shows the weekly range for the same average and period, and clarifies the picture.[4] (See page 27, paragraph 3, of the Treatise.) My next Letter will discuss the immediate technical effect on equities of the present status of Federal Securities, the Triangular Outline, and the Corporate Bond thrust.

Bull Markets: Bull markets enjoy powerful technical support throughout and disregard economic errors, which will be reflected in the subsequent bear market. Note the attached graph of the last bull market of 1932-1937.[5] During the entire five year period, there was no deviation from the law of precedents as revealed in the Treatise. See page 24, paragraphs 1 and 2. The movement from March to November 1938 was not a bull market, although its pattern was a perfect cycle as shown in Letter No. 1. Orthodox bull markets are usually widely separated.

Bear Markets: Ordinarily, bear markets last longer than bull markets.[6] See Treatise, page 37. Bear markets, especially their rallies, are erratic and occasionally treacherous. Political attempts to correct errors committed during the previous bull market and the current bear market often make conditions worse. Temporary bear market reversals may be due to some technical influence such as, for example, the action of corporate bonds. See Letter No. 7.

R.N. Elliott

FOOTNOTES

[1] Great call.

[2] This entire analysis is wonderful and exactly correct, although Elliott abandons it later.

[3] This explanation and wave labeling indicate that Elliott had a good deal of difficulty changing his!

[4] Except that he has repositioned the wave labels.

[5] See Educational Bulletin A, from which his enclosure (not shown here) was reproduced.

[6] Although this happens occasionally, it does not happen "ordinarily." In fact, it is almost never true in the stock market, as Elliott's own wave interpretations prove. See discussion in Chapter 4 of *Elliott Wave Principle*.

CONFIDENTIAL

September 6, 1939

The recent technical situation has been more complicated and interesting than any other period within my observation. I believe it is not an exaggeration to say that only by familiarity with The Wave Principle would it be possible to understand and appreciate the significance of the indications. On the attached page will be found six charts (**U**, **V**, **W**, **X**, **Y**, **Z**) of varying factors and influence, but all related.

Z The Dow Jones Industrial Average bottomed at 120.04 on April 11, and its 3rd wave upward topped at 145.75 on July 18. Wave 1 of this movement was exceedingly slow and deceptive as described in the Letter of May 27. If this delay had not occurred the average could easily have reached a much higher figure and completed 5 waves by July 18. This delay permitted the business cycle, graph **W**, which started a month earlier, to overtake the Dow Jones Industrial Average, and wave 3 of both business and equity cycles reached top about the same time July 18. Both then made a sidewise movement (flat) simultaneously; note the two charts. The business cycle entered its 5th wave and still continues its advance, but wave C of the Dow Jones Industrials developed a serious decline, a distortion which was occasioned by the London Industrial Average, graph **Y**, which began a bearish triangle on January 26 at 91.4, reaching its apex at 101.4 on July 28, from which point it was due to register a downward thrust in 5 waves with a bottom which I forecast in my Letter of August 17 would approximate 88 in early September.[1] It reached 92.4 on August 24. Since August 31, the London Stock Exchange has been closed.

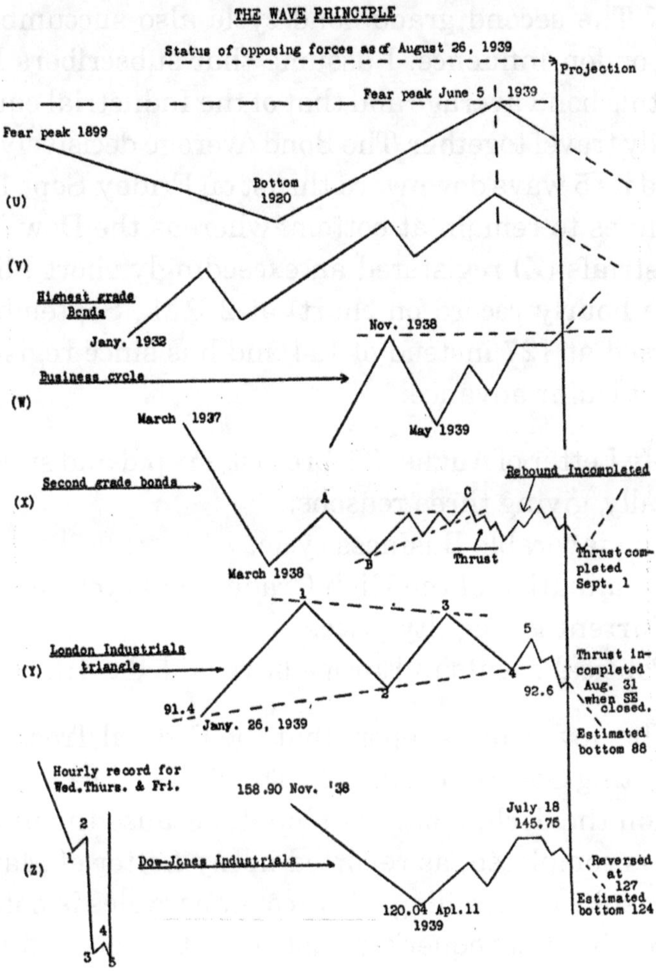

Ordinarily, I would not have attached any particular importance to this technical feature as affecting our market, but presuming the cause of the bearish triangle signal to be threat of war, I intimated in my Letter of August 17[2] that the Dow Jones Industrial Average might abandon its bullish indications and synchronize with the London market. This proved correct, as reported August 26.[2] At the same time I forecast approximately 124[3] as the probable bottom of the Dow Jones Industrials.

X The second grade bond cycle also succumbed to the London influence. I assume that subscribers know that this bond average and that of the Industrial equities usually travel together. The Bond Average decisively completed its 5 wave downward thrust on Friday, Sept 1, and continues to remain at bottom, whereas the Dow Jones Industrials (**Z**) registered an exceedingly short Minute 5 (see hourly record on chart) at 2 P.M., September 1, reversed at 127 instead of 124 and has since registered a spectacular advance.

My Letter of August 26 forecast a rapid and substantial rally, giving three reasons:

The favorable Business cycle,
Termination of the High Grade Bond cycle, and
Current low equity prices.
Political events in Europe have added a 4th reason.

The newspapers report that the Federal Treasury is supporting Government bonds. The Treasury can possibly cushion the decline but not stop it, because the upward cycle is completed, as reported in my Letter of May 27. The results of meddling with economic cycles is noted in the British Exchequer's disastrous attempt to support pound sterling.

Respectfully submitted,

R.N. Elliott

FOOTNOTES

[1] A good forecast. See Footnote 7 in Interpretive Letter No. 9.

[2] Neither of these Forecast Letters is available.

[3] Another good call.

INTERPRETIVE LETTER No. 9

April 11 to September 13, 1939

A rare and important technical situation occurred recently when the action of the London Industrials influenced to the point of domination the action of the New York market.[1] This is fully described in my Confidential Letter of September 6 and sheet of charts showing "Status of opposing forces as of August 26, 1939," enclosed herewith. A similar instance of dominating influence by one average was described in Interpretive Letter No. 7.

Shown on the next page are the charts of the Dow Jones and London Industrial Averages.

Graph **R** is the weekly range of the Dow Jones Industrials from April 11 to September 13, 1939.

Graph **S** is the daily range of waves 2 and 3,[2] with "flat,"[3] "thrust"[4] and "rebound" to September 13. Wave 1 is represented by a straight line, the detailed daily range of which was minutely described in Interpretive Letter No. 8.

Graph **T** is an orthodox triangle seen in the London Industrials, and attention is invited to the date (July 28) when the *apex* (*end of the 5th wave*) occurred, and its relation to the Dow Jones Industrials. In that period, the Dow Jones Industrials formed waves A and B of a flat, preparatory for wave 5. Wave C of the flat should have ended around 140. This is the first time in my observation that a flat failed to produce a continuation of the previous movement (wave 3). Wave 2 was a zigzag. Zigzags and flats usually alternate. Note 4th paragraph of letter of September 6, attached.

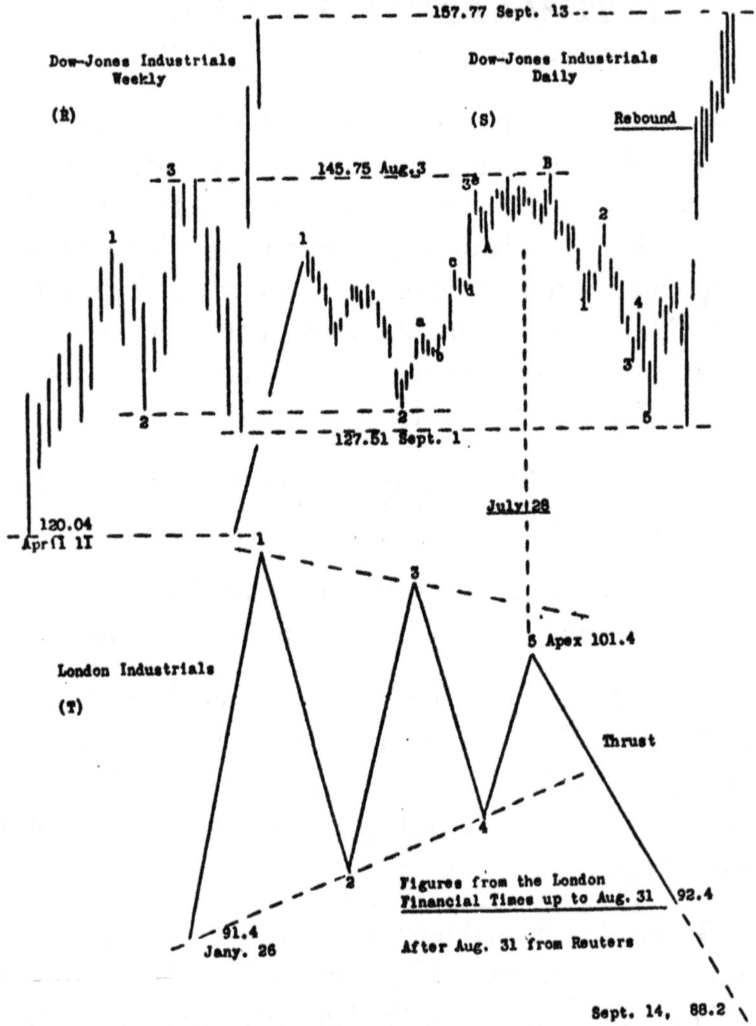

In the London Industrials, the movement below the apex to 88 is a "thrust." As New York synchronized with London, we must call the decline of the Dow Jones Industrials from B to 5 a "thrust."[5] The movement subsequent to "thrusts" is a "rebound."[6] The violence of the Dow Jones rebound was due to four causes described in the Letter of September 6 (near bottom) and forecast in the Letter of August 26.

The London Industrial Average is now around the bottom of 88 forecast in the Letter of August 17, the rebound in that index not yet having started.[7]

R.N. Elliott

FOOTNOTES

[1] Actually, the market had merely peaked in a "B" wave of a flat which began at the peak of Elliott's wave 1. See Footnote 2.

[2] Obviously this cannot be wave 3, since wave 4 deeply overlaps wave 1. See Footnote 11 for Interpretive Letter No. 1. Clearly the best interpretation of the move from the top of wave 1 to the bottom on September 1 is that the entire structure is a flat correction composing wave 2. He adopts the correct interpretation in Interpretive Letter No. 11, just in time to make a great market call.

[3] Elliott's flat has a far too elongated wave C, a habit which produced odd counts for tops in 1929 and 1937 as well. In this particular instance, he leaves off the label for wave C (which should go below the 5), possibly because of the new low seven trading days later. Elliott alludes to some of these structural problems in the next paragraph.

[4] Here Elliott uses the term "thrust" incorrectly to refer to wave C of a flat.

[5] Under Elliott's definition of thrust, the decline in the U.S. market most certainly is not one. What is clearly true for the London market is not necessarily so for the U.S. market or any other. Elliott reverses his opinion on this point a short time later. See Interpretive Letter No. 15, Footnote 1.

[6] Apart from the first reference on chart **X** of the Forecast Letter of September 6 (labeled "Confidential"), this is the only time that Elliott uses this term.

[7] It did, just days later, a great call by Elliott.

INTERPRETIVE LETTER No. 10

September 1 to October 26, 1939

W The graph on the next page is the D-J Industrials. Between September 13 and October 9, a horizontal symmetrical triangle is shown, as described in the Treatise on page 21, paragraph 3C. This triangle forecast a small thrust upward of five waves, following the apex on October 9. Thrusts have always been fast, and a failure had never before been noted. This thrust was slow, and the 5th vibration of the 5th wave failed, as indicated by the dashed line.[1] See Treatise, page 20, paragraph 2.

XYZ These graphs cover the same period as **W** and all are different in outline.

Z Is a private average of Industrials. The outline is a flat bottomed triangle as described in the Treatise on page 21, paragraph 3B. In composition, the legs are orthodox but the outline is slightly imperfect in that leg 2 penetrates the upper line, though this is of no importance.[2] The thrust failed to complete and the subsequent action appears even weaker than the D-J Industrials.[3]

Y D-J Rails resembles the D-J Industrials in the composition of the waves during the triangle period but the outline is entirely abortive.

X Action of Composite 2nd Grade Bonds also resembles that of the Industrial averages during the triangle, i.e. the composition of waves in both directions. After leaving the triangle period, the thrust developed satisfactorily, although with no excess enthusiasm. Note the contacts with the channel at C1 to C5.

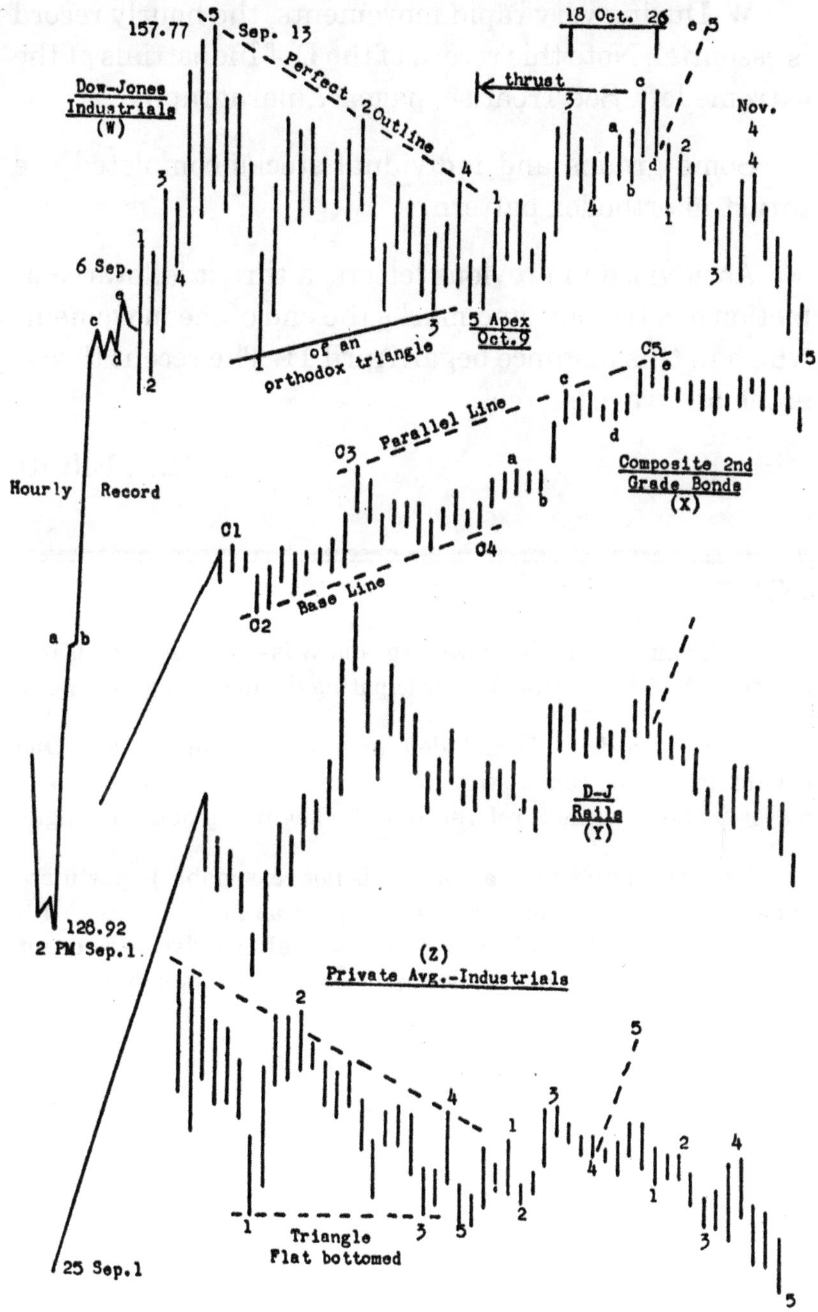
157.77
Sep. 13
Perfect Outline
Dow-Jones Industrials (W)
18 Oct. 26
thrust
Nov.
6 Sep.
5 Apex Oct.9
of an orthodox triangle
Parallel Line
Base Line
Composite 2nd Grade Bonds (X)
Hourly Record
D-J Rails (Y)
126.92
2 PM Sep.1
(Z)
Private Avg.-Industrials
Triangle Flat bottomed
25 Sep.1

W During very rapid movements, the hourly record is essential. Note this record of the D-J Industrials at the extreme left. See Treatise, page 27, paragraph 3.

Some groups and individual stocks completed the thrust in orthodox pattern.

As advised in previous letters, a thrust follows completion of a triangle and marks the end of the movement, which in this instance began April 11. The recent thrust is the 5th wave thereof.

R.N. Elliott

FOOTNOTES

[1] The interpretation shown in graph **W** is excellent, and his recognition of a failure critical to anticipating the upcoming weakness.

[2] True. Frost and I concluded the same thing in our book. One should obtain the correct triangle lines by connecting the ends of waves 2 and 4, without reference to the beginning of the triangle.

[3] As with previous examples, it is not reasonable to postulate such sizable missing or incomplete waves as he illustrates with dashed lines on charts **Y** and **Z**. A better alternative is to count acceptably whatever the market has provided by its action.

INTERPRETIVE LETTER No. 11

October 25, 1939 to January 3, 1940[1]

Below are shown four graphs, **W, X, Y, Z.**

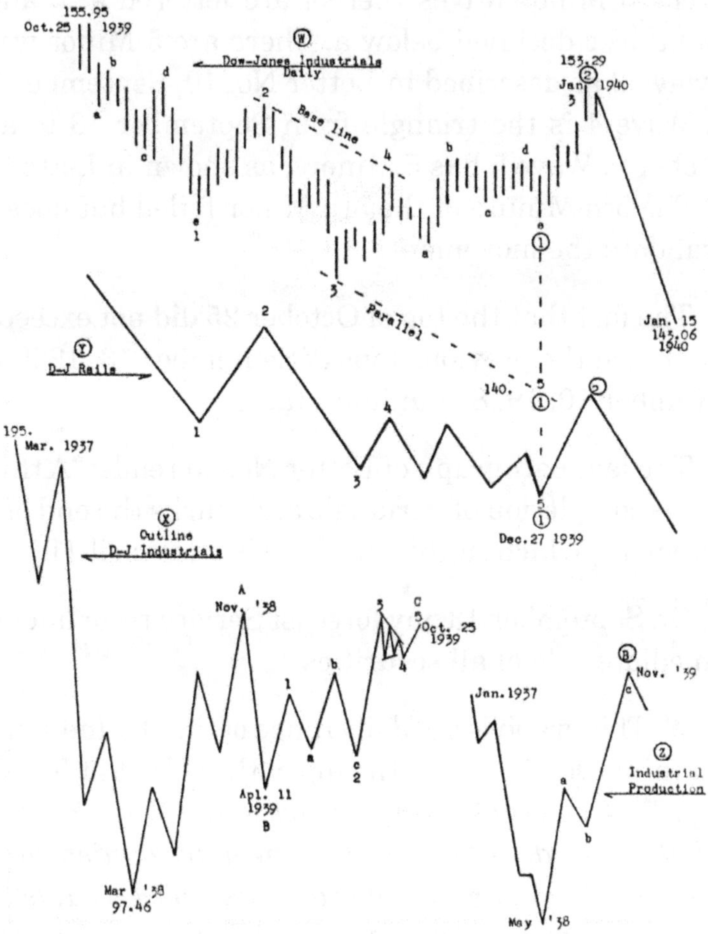

X Outlines the DJ Industrials from March 10, 1937 to October 25, 1939.[2] Note the zigzag pattern in Treatise, page 17, paragraph 1, fig. A. Wave B of fig. B furnishes details of the picture more in consonance with the movement between March 1938 and October 25, 1939. *The*

main outline of all corrections is always the same. Wave B to C, graph **X**, April 11 to October 25, 1939, may require some clarification. Attention is invited to page 16 of the Treatise, paragraphs 2 and 3. Wave B is an "irregular" type shown on page 16 of the Treatise, paragraph 3, fig. C. The 3 Minor waves thereof are lettered a, b and c. Note that c declined below a. There are 5 Minor waves in wave 3 as described in Letter No. 10, September 1 to 13. Wave 4 is the triangle from September 13 to apex October 9. Wave 5 has 5 Minors, as shown in Letter No. 10. The 5th Minute of the 5th Minor failed but does not invalidate the movement.

The fact that the top of October 25 did not exceed, or even reach the previous tops of September 13, 1939 and November 10, 1938 is unimportant.

The last paragraph of Letter No. 10 reads: "A thrust follows completion of a triangle and marks the end of the movement, which in this instance began April 11."

On September 13, my forecast Service recommended immediate sale of all securities.[3]

W This graph is the daily range of the D-J Industrials beginning October 25 at the top of the thrust at 5 of C in graph **X**. *One of the many virtues of the Wave Principle is that the student knows when the market misbehaves, which is seldom, and insofar as I have observed, is confined to rallies of Bear Markets.*[4] See last paragraph of Letter No. 8. Note the correct pattern of wave 5 of the Rails, graph **Y**, then compare with the same period of the Industrials immediately above. The figure 5 at the intersection of the two dashed lines represents the point to which it was expected the Industrials would decline on December 27, 1939 (140). The Minor waves of the Industrials, a to e, were correct in number and position, but a, c and e refused to behave. Nevertheless I consider December 27 as the end of wave ① (counting from October 25).[5] From December 27 to January 3 at 153.29 is wave ②. From ② downward is the beginning of wave ③.

Z This graph is an outline of the Industrial Production during the same period as **X** and **W**. It is an "irregular" pattern as shown in the Treatise page 16, paragraph 3, in that B is slightly higher than the beginning of A.

This Letter is issued long before it is due, but the sidewise movement has consumed so much time that subscribers may become anxious for interpretations. You may be interested in the hint given in my Forecast Letter of November 21[3] which reads in part as follows:

> "Two notable examples of long indecision have occurred:
>
> 1. Between January and June of 1904, 5 months, within a range of 4.09 points. See Treatise page 24, paragraph 3.
>
> 2. Between October 1909 and July 1914, 5 years, within a range of 28 points.[6]
>
> Both of these are traceable to politics."

R.N. Elliott

FOOTNOTES

[1] Elliott began his Educational Service during this time.

[2] The labeling on this chart is exactly right. Elliott has shifted to the correct a-b-c irregular flat count for wave 2, and has concluded that a larger A-B-C ended on October 25. This is a brilliant call on the market, anticipating a major decline which materialized in the form of the May 1940 crash.

[3] No copy of this page survives.

[4] A excellent practical observation.

[5] I consider this observation untenable. It is common for one of the two averages to register an orthodox top or bottom at a different time from the other, setting up a nonconfirmation at the second peak or low.

[6] This period of "long indecision" resolved in a market collapse and war. Elliott's commentary comes quite close to forecasting a market crash based on war, which is exactly what is to occur four months from this date.

INTERPRETIVE LETTER No. 12

October 25, 1939 to April 8, 1940

The movement from the top of the thrust, October 25, 1939, to April 8, 1940, is unusually interesting and instructive on account of certain rare patterns and the extremely narrow range, 13 points during five months. My analysis of the causes is covered in the attached special letter, dated April 1, 1940, entitled "The Current Situation in the Stock Market."[1]

Graph U portrays the Dow Jones Industrial average. Downward wave (1) covers the period from October 25 to January 15, which is subdivided into 5 waves of lesser degree.[2] Of these, wave 4 is a "double 3," which has the same significance as an ordinary "single 3".[3] Graph W is a simple outline of this type of correction. The unusual feature of this wave 4 is its duration, which equals that of the preceding three waves. Upward corrective wave (2) covers the period from January 15 to April 8.[4] The pattern is an upward "zigzag," that is, 5 up, 3 down and 5 up, the reverse of Figure A, paragraph 1, page 17 of the Treatise. The duration was extremely long. See graph **X**.

Graph **V** portrays the Dow Jones Rail average. From October 25 to January 15, this average completed 5 waves downward. Of these, the 3rd extended to December 27 at 30.78. This extension was "double-retraced" by waves 4 and 5. From January 15 to April 8, an inverted "irregular" flat followed, i.e., 3 up, 3 down and 5 up, all of which formed wave (2). This pattern is the reverse of the last figure on page 16 of the Treatise. See graph **Y**.

R.N. Elliott

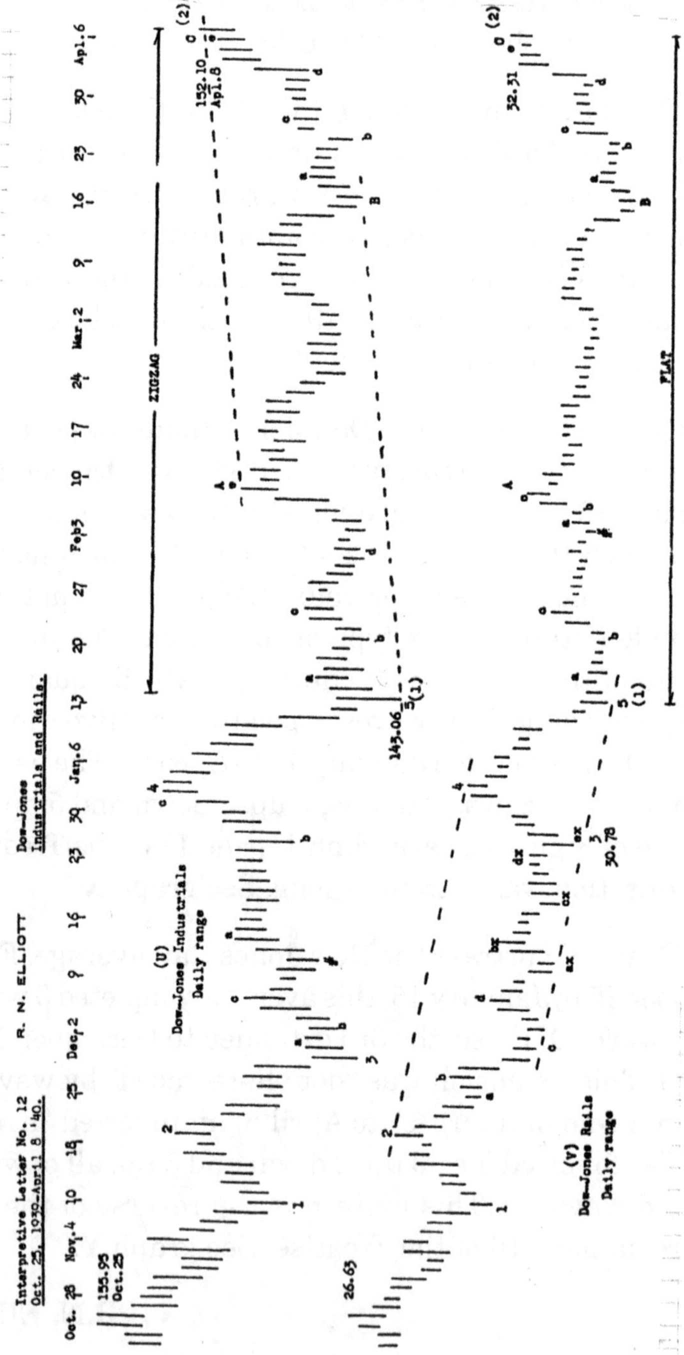

Interpretive Letter No. 12
Oct. 25, 1939-April 8 '40.
R. N. ELLIOTT
Dow-Jones
Industrials and Rails.
(U)
Dow-Jones Industrials
Daily range
(V)
Dow-Jones Rails
Daily range
ZIGZAG
FLAT
155.95
Oct.25
143.06
152.10
Apl.8
26.63
30.78
32.31

(X)

ZIGZAG

Correction of upward trends

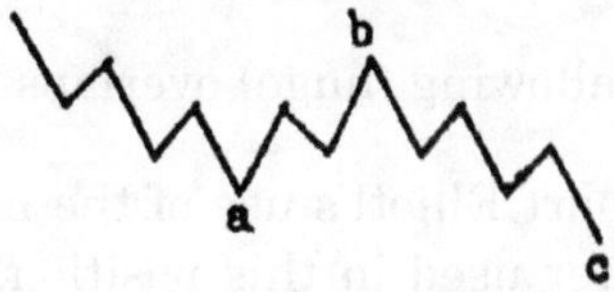

Correction of down trends

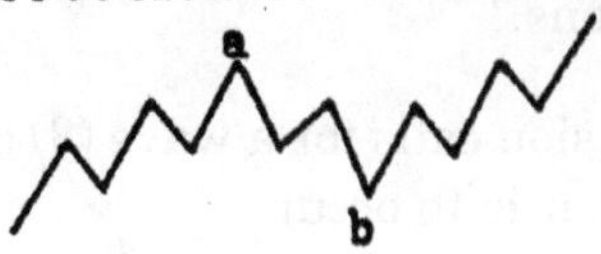

(W)

"DOUBLE 3"

Correction of upward trends

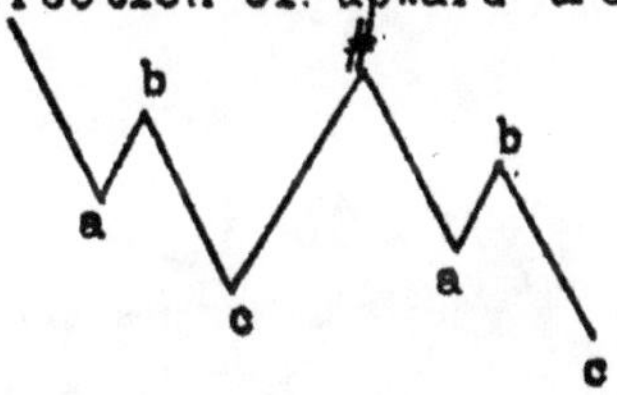

Correction of down trends

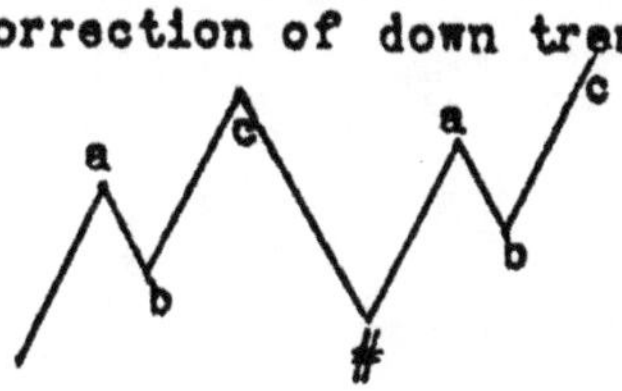

(Y)

"IRREGULAR" FLAT Inverted

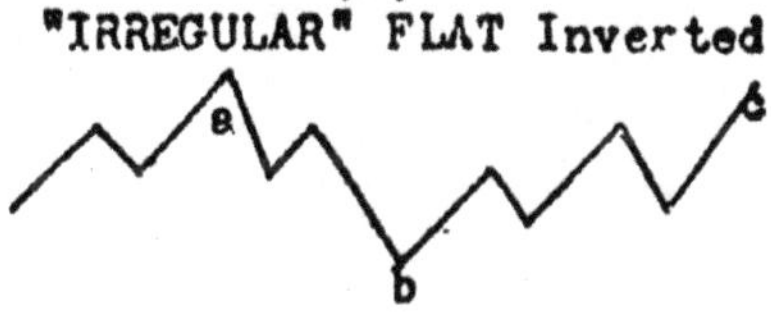

FOOTNOTES

[1] One of the Educational Bulletins, not available.

[2] Elliott is still allowing (huge) overlaps at this point.

[3] Note on the chart Elliott's use of the number sign in place of the "x" that he later used in this position. He will later label this formation a "double zigzag," saving the "double three" label for sideways corrections.

[4] Elliott's conclusion calls for a wave (3) crash directly ahead, which is precisely what is to occur.

INTERPRETIVE LETTER No. 13

April 8 to June 18, 1940

Graph **W1** portrays waves (1), (2), (3) and (4) from of the Industrials October 25, 1939 to June 18, 1940, which follow graph **X** of Letter No. 11.

Graph **W2** portrays the daily range of waves (3) and (4), which follow waves (1) and (2) of graph **(U)** of Letter No. 12. The details of waves (3) and (4) are very important and require careful study. The Minute waves of Minor wave (3) are discernible, but should have reached a much lower point. The Minute waves of Minor wave 5, ending May 15 at 125.76, are discernible only on the hourly record as shown in graph **W3**. This is due to the high speed. Minor wave 5 extended in minute 5; note xa, xb, xc, xd and xe.[1]

Graph **W2** covers wave (4) from May 15 to June 18. This wave started and ended at about the same level. The pattern is of the "flat" type shown in the Treatise on page 17, paragraph 1, which, for convenient reference, is shown under **Z1**. This pattern applies to upward trends. **Z2** is inverted and therefore applies to downward trends. **Z3** is the same pattern as **Z2** except that wave b thereof is elongated. An actual demonstration of same is shown in wave 4 on page 46 of the Treatise. *Always keep in mind that the length of waves varies, but seldom their number, which is the fundamental virtue of The Wave Principle.*

W2 The pattern of the movement across the bottom (between B and 2) is so exceedingly rare that no mention thereof appears in the Treatise. The details baffle any count.[2] However, the first "exposed contact" is at 2, as shown on page 7, paragraph 1 of the Treatise.

X Rails. This average topped at 26.76 on June 28, ten days later than the Industrials (June 18) because of an extension, which has subsequently been double-retraced.

Y Utilities. This average registered much the same bottom as the Industrials and is therefore counted in the same manner across the bottom. It then extended and double-retraced as described in the Treatise on page 18, paragraph 4. The highest point thereof, thus far, occurred at 23.92 on June 28, the same date as the Rails.

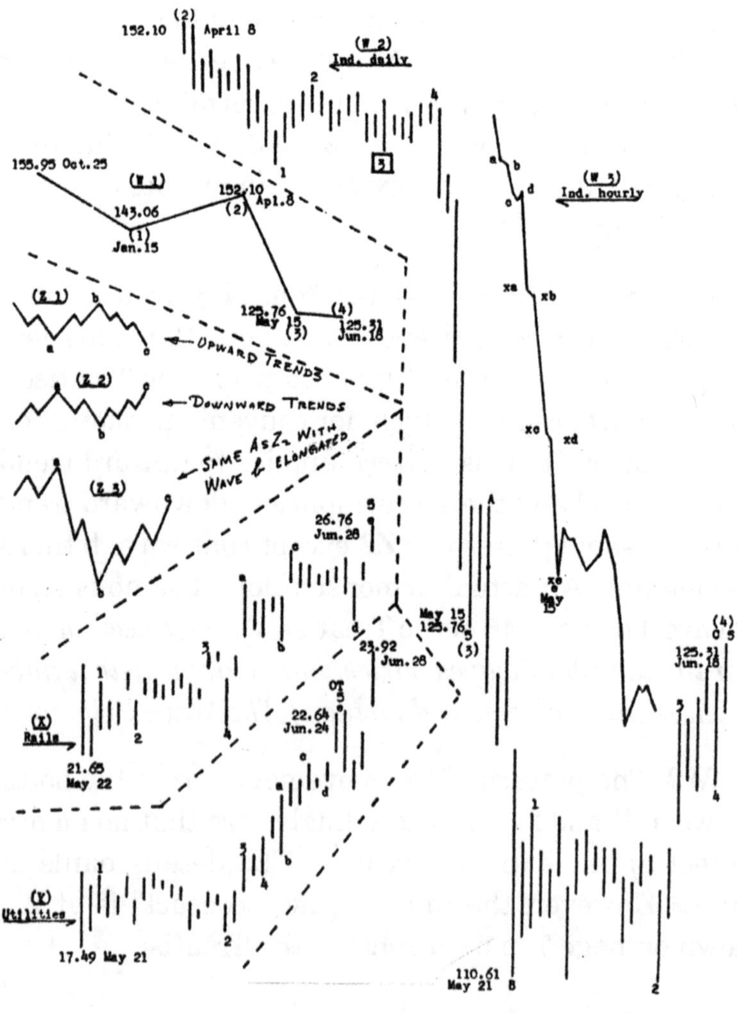

This extension occurred just previous to Mr. Willkie's nomination. The second retracement registered the day following his nomination, June 28, at 23.92.

Corporate bonds. Previous Letters have described the influence of corporate bonds over equities. This influence has been much in evidence since October 1939. Up to July 19, this index extended, and recovered 82% of its decline from April 8 to May 21. This subject will be fully discussed in a subsequent Letter.[3]

Insofar as records are available (daily range 1928), an extension has never occurred in direction opposite to the current main trend,[4] *therefore further developments will have to define what the implications may be.*

Economic and political dislocations are more extensive and serious today than ever before.

R.N. Elliott

FOOTNOTES

[1] This internal wave count is a mess, for one reason. Elliott has a powerful bias toward counting extensions in fifth waves rather than third waves. This labeling tendency is understandable in that the two great bull markets of Elliott's lifetime, 1921-1929 and 1932-1937, had extended fifths. He obviously concluded that they were typical, when in fact third waves extend far more often (see *Elliott Wave Principle*). Counting an extended third here provides a beautiful and simple interpretation. His extended fifth results in further problems in his description of the very large irregular wave (4). The chart on the next page is the best interpretation.

[2] It's not rare at all, but clearly a contracting triangle followed by a fifth wave thrust to the orthodox bottom where Elliott has labeled his wave 2 (see chart on the next page).

[3] The next one, in fact.

[4] As well as I can discern, Elliott is referring to movements three degrees lower than the main trend. I.e., wave i, iii or v of wave a or c of wave 2 or 4 within a larger five wave sequence should not be an extension.

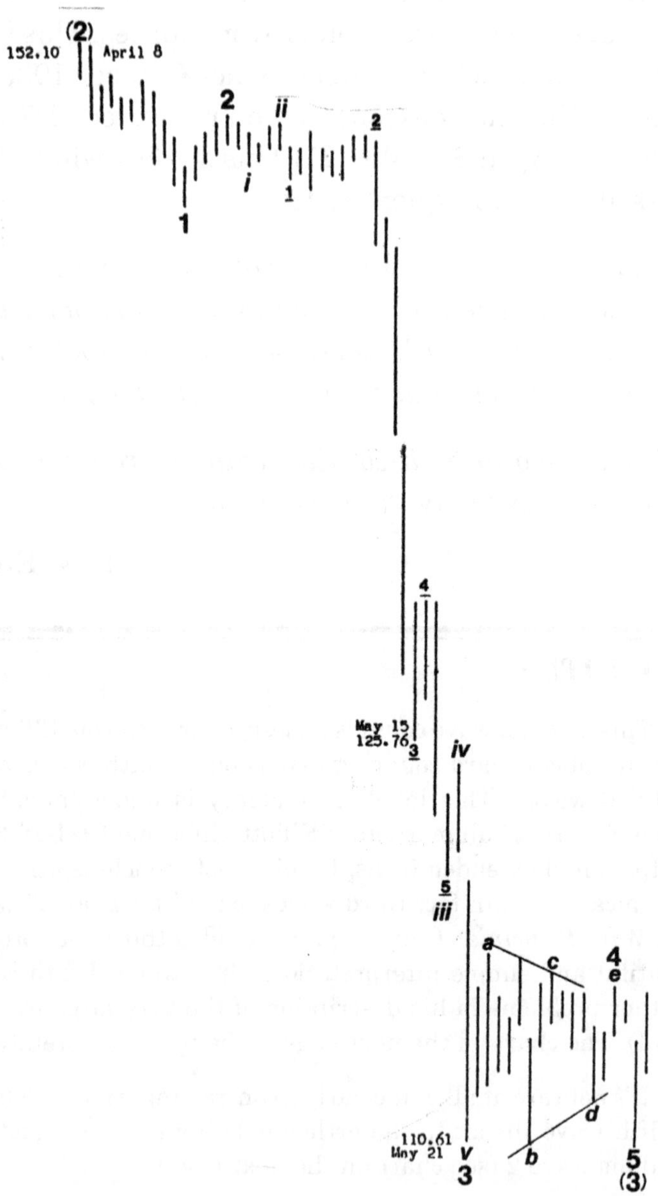

INTERPRETIVE LETTER No. 14

May 21 to June 18 and
June 18 to October 3, 1940

In order to demonstrate the buoyancy of Corporate Bonds (graph **V**)and their influence over equities, the chart herewith repeats the movement shown in Letter No. 13, from May 21 to June 18, wave (4), as well as that from June 18 to October 3, 1940.1

Between June 18 and July 25 (indicated by a horizontal line underneath the Industrial index, graph **W**), this influence became impelling. The scheduled cyclical and final decline of the bear market (wave 5^1) failed to materialize. The five weeks sideways movement was devoid of pattern, a feature never before noted.[2]

Between April 1934 and March 1937, Corporate Bonds were "out of gear" with equities and exerted no influence. As Bonds are again "out of gear," it may be that their influence has terminated. Resumption of pattern since July 25 apparently confirms this presumption.

Another feature meriting close attention is the appearance of numerous extensions during June and August, that is, previous to, and following the period during which there was no pattern. In itself, this circumstance is important as it confirms that a decline should have registered in July. Extensions do not repeat in a single movement; that is, in a 5 wave movement, only one of the three impulses (1, 3 or 5) will extend. Therefore, the extensions of Rails (graph **X**) and Utilities in June cannot belong to the same cyclical movement as those of August. Extensions occurred during June in the Rails, Utilities and Corporate Bonds. During August, extensions registered in the Rails, Utilities and Industrials.

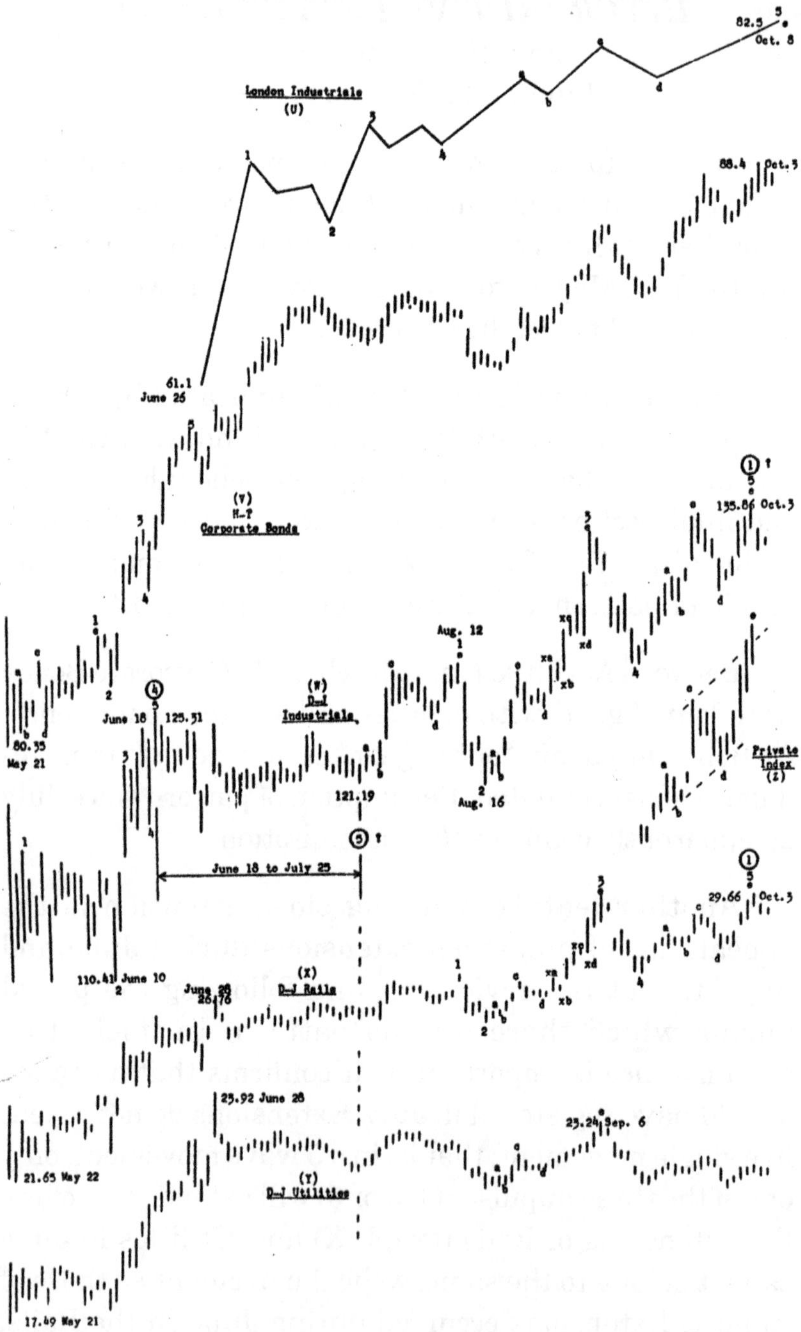

London Industrials
(U)
61.1
June 25
82.5
Oct. 8
(V)
N-Y
Corporate Bonds
88.4
Oct.3
(W)
D-J
Industrials
80.35
May 21
June 18
125.31
121.19
Aug. 12
Aug. 16
135.86
Oct.3
Private
Index
(Z)
June 18 to July 25
110.41
June 10
(X)
D-J Rails
June 28
26.76
29.66
Oct.3
21.65 May 22
25.92 June 28
25.24
Sep. 6
(Y)
D-J Utilities
17.49 May 21

From July 25 to October 3, the three equity averages registered five waves upward. While not all patterns are well formed, return to normalcy is apparent. Graph **Z** shows a perfect pattern for wave 5 in a private industrial average that I consider superior to all the popular indices, due to its scientific construction.

Graph **U** shows the London Industrials from June 26 to October 8 (61.1 to 82.5) in five waves, which confirms my advice of July 9[3] to Forecast subscribers to the effect that the bear market low had passed. In 1932 and 1937, London reversed one and two months, respectively, ahead of New York. On this basis, too, New York should have bottomed in July or August.

The evidence thus far available inclines me to assume, tentatively, that our bear market terminated July 25.[4] This would not preclude the possibility of a subsequent normal correction below the figure which registered on that date, 121.19.[5]

Because of the absence of pattern during June and July, I was compelled to withhold release of this Letter.[6]

R.N. Elliott

FOOTNOTES

[1] This wave is labeled with a circle on the chart in this letter.

[2] Actually, there is no missing fifth wave. The decline was simply a "three" because it is wave (b) of a large triangle wave Ⓑ that ultimately covers the period from March 1938 to July 1941. It is a tricky move by the market, however, and most analysts would have had trouble here.

[3] Not available.

[4] Elliott is now proceeding under the assumption that a new bull market is in force, when in fact it is merely a bear market rally (wave (c) of a triangle). By his own description, five waves down does not indicate the end of a correction. There was an unmistakable five wave decline from 1937 to the 1938 low, yet Elliott ignores his own basic rule and begins to encounter many points of difficulty as a result. His resulting errors do not detract from the Wave Principle's value. On the contrary, they support it, since the low of that five wave structure, after a Fibonacci 62% retracement, was broken, as required. Had the market behaved otherwise, in line with its discoverer's bias, the principle itself might have been violated. It is well to keep in mind that Elliott had been practicing this application for only a short while at this point, and firm conviction regarding rules probably had yet to be fully established in his mind.

[5] It is not clear why a normal correction in a new bull market would go below the orthodox low of the bear market. Elliott is probably just hedging his bet that the low is in place, which is based on "a feature never before noted."

[6] Until October 3, as per the heading on the letter.

INTERPRETIVE LETTER No. 15

July 25 to November 8, 1940

Below you will find graphs of the daily range of the Averages and that of U.S. Steel from July 25 to November 8. No two are harmonious.[1] U.S. Steel exhibited unusual strength and this strength, was also seen in the Coppers. The Industrial average is next in strength because of the presence therein of stocks from these groups. The Rails

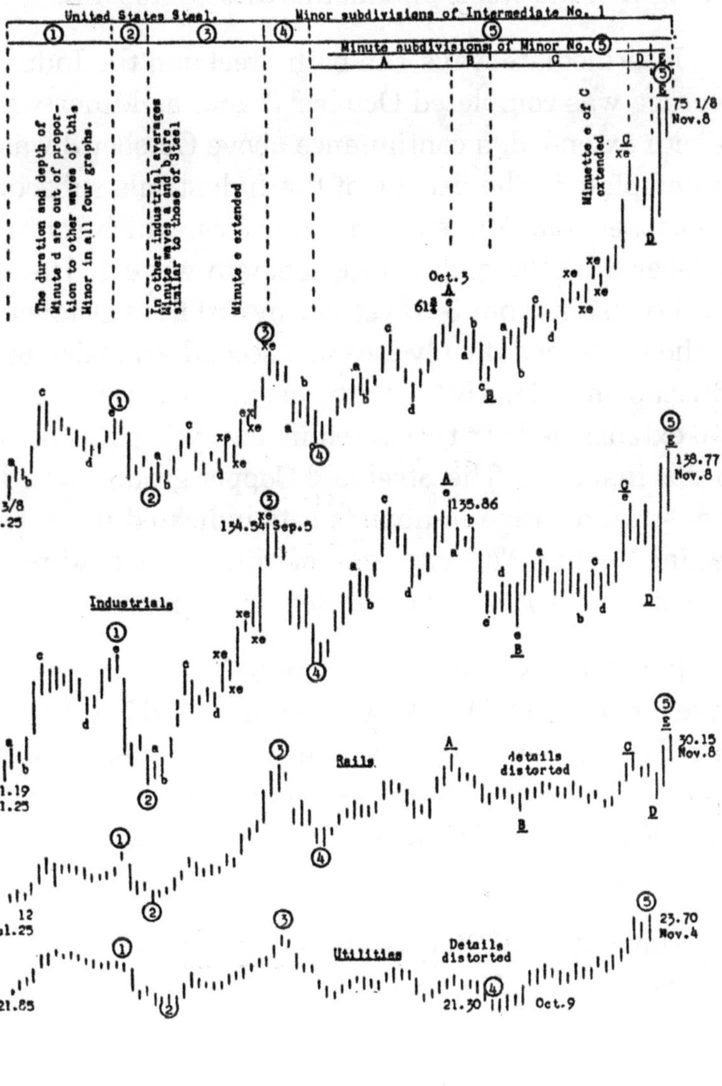

barely held their own and the Utilities moved sidewise in an imperfect pattern.

In Letter No. 14, the ending of Intermediate wave 1 of the Industrial average is shown at October 3 with a question mark. This uncertainty was due to the questionable ending of Intermediate wave 5 of the late bear market, likewise shown with a question mark. This uncertainty was dissipated in an unexpected manner, i.e., the unusual strength of the steels and metals after October 3.

Intermediate wave 1 in both Steel and the Industrial average was completed October 3 and, as Minor wave 3 of both extended, a continuance above October 3 was not contemplated. The decline of the Industrials subsequent to October 3 at A has 5 Minute waves, which confirmed October 3 as the end of Intermediate wave 1. However, Steel registered but 3 waves downward from October 3 at A, then resumed its advance in a second extension of this Intermediate. This is the first time in my observation that two extensions ever registered in one cycle (Intermediate in this instance). The Steel and Copper groups forced the Industrial average to abandon its indicated intention to decline further. The extension of Minuette e of Minute C, an extension within an extension, is not new.

Incidentally, wave E of Minor 5 (November 8) should have registered 5 Minute waves and added 5 to 10 points to U.S. Steel, but only one Minute developed. A private average, in which I have reason to place great confidence and designate as "Scientific," did register 5 Minute waves up to November 14.

The pattern of Steel is a replica of graph 5, paragraph 2, page 17 of the Treatise.

Exhaustive research of all available records does not disclose any similar abnormalities to those of the past six months, such as:

a. Omission of an intermediate wave (No. 5 of the late bear market)

b. Two extensions in one intermediate (Steel)

c. Distortion of patterns of the averages.[2]

Only The Wave Principle reveals these features.

Letter No. 13 said: "Economic and political dislocations are more extensive and serious today than ever before."

R.N. Elliott

FOOTNOTES

[1] Nor need they be. Each market develops its own waves, as its informational feedback loop affects and is created by a different, albeit similar, group of people.

[2] Despite the discussion in this letter, the best interpretation of the rally from June 10, 1940 is that of a triple zigzag. See illustration below.

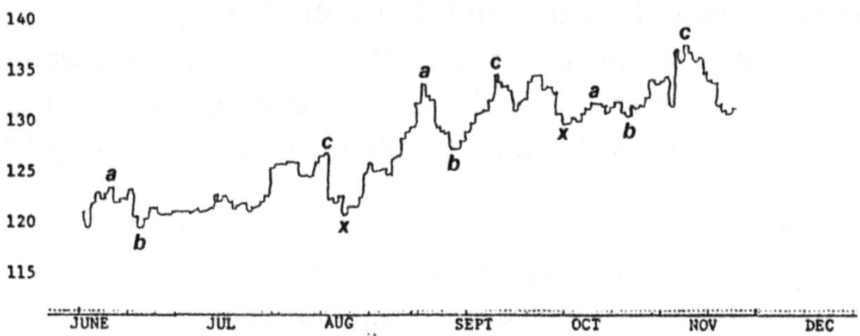

INTERPRETIVE LETTER No. 16

November 8/14, 1940 to February 19, 1941

The previous Letter, No. 15, showed November 8 at 138.77 as the top of Intermediate wave 1, whereas subsequent market action demonstrates that the orthodox top occurred on November 14 at 137.78.

On the next page are shown graphs **Y** and **Z**. The former is the daily range of the Dow Jones Industrial Index. The latter portrays the Herald-Tribune Bond Index. Both cover the same period, November 14, 1940 to February 19, 1941.

Recent Letters discussed extensions, whereas the feature of this Letter is the "double 3" pattern, which made its first appearance during 1939 and is described in Letter No. 12. It may have occurred previous to 1928, when the daily range was inaugurated. Being corrective, it would be confined to the smaller degrees visible only in the daily range.[1] As previously reported, the "double 3" has precisely the same significance as a single 3.

Graph **Y**, *D-J Industrials*: The first downward movement completed 5 waves at "a", thus demonstrating that the orthodox top occurred November 14. It also indicated that the minimum correction would be a "zigzag." (See Treatise, page 17, paragraph 1, graph A). A zigzag pattern was completed on December 23 at "A", but evidence of climactic character was absent. The subsequent advance reached "B" at 134.27 January 10 in 7 waves, a "double 3."

Between November 14 and January 10, we have now seen 3 down and 3 up,[2] or an "A B" top[3] which calls for 5 down as described in the last graph on page 16. However, as the "double 3" pattern has been quite common of late, the student should be prepared for an enlarged "Double 3" at 122.29 February 4. On arrival at that point, no evidence of final bottom developed; therefore, 5 waves down from January 10 was to be expected, thus completing a "flat." (See last pattern on page 16). Climactic behavior developed February 14, terminating at 117.64. This was the 3rd wave down from February 6. The 5th wave down registered February 19 at 117.43, thus ending Intermediate wave 2.[4] When waves 1 and 2 are very small and wave 3 long, then waves 4 and 5 will be similar to waves 1 and 2. (See page 17, paragraph 2, graph wave 3, inverted.)

Graph **Z**, *Corporate Bonds*: The entire pattern is "corrective" and a "double 3." From November 14 to "A"

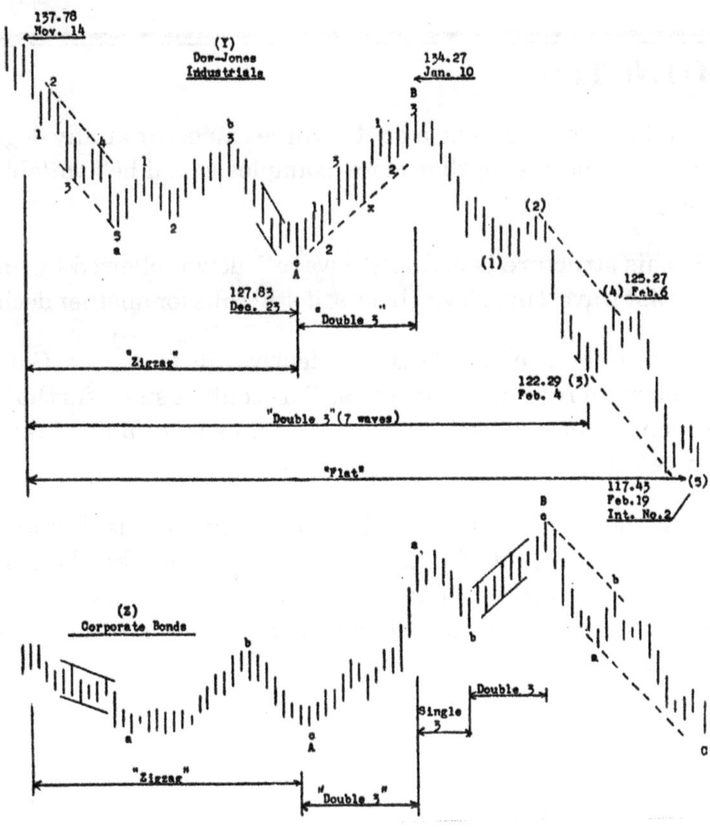

is a "zigzag." Each of the three movements, A, B and C, is composed of 3 waves. Movement "B", with two "double 3s" separated by a single 3, is novel but strictly orthodox and the same behavior may occur any time in an equity average group or individual stock. Note that this extended double 3 appears in "new territory" (above the top of last November), and in direction of the current main trend (upward), all of which complies with rules of extensions. In detail and in the whole, the picture indicates strength.

Note that the 9 movements of each graph start and end simultaneously with each other.

R.N. Elliott

FOOTNOTES

[1] Like all corrections, a double three can occur at any degree. Elliott might be saying that more examples would be available in the daily range chart.

[2] This structure is actually a wave 1 down followed by an irregular flat wave 2 up. Nevertheless, it still calls for another decline.

[3] The reference to an "AB top" clearly calls for a wave C down to complete an irregular correction. This context suggests that his later mention in "Nature's Law" of an "AB base" could be taken in the same context.

[4] As the market falls lower in subsequent months, Elliott will abandon the interpretation that a new bull market has begun. In order to explain the corrective behavior of most of this period, he switches to his interpretation that a triangle has been in force since 1929.

INTERPRETIVE LETTER No. 17
Two Cycles of American History[1]

August 25, 1941

1776 - 1857, 81 years
1857 - 1941, 84 years

The earliest available stock record is the Axe-Houghton Index, dating from 1854. The essential "change" characteristics of the long movement from 1854 to September, 1929 are shown in the accompanying graph. The wave from 1857 to 1929 may be either Cycle wave I, III or V, depending upon the nature and extent of development of the country before 1854. There is reason to believe, however, that the period from 1857 to 1929 can be regarded as Cycle wave III.[2] In the first place, the broad periodicity of approximately eighty years connects the Revolutionary Period, the Civil War Period and World War II that has been in progress during the past decade. Secondly, the market since 1929 has outlined the pattern of a gigantic thirteen-year triangle of such tremendous scope that these defeatist years may well be grouped as Cycle wave IV. Thirdly, my observation has been that orthodox triangles appear only as the fourth wave of a cycle.

To appreciate the cause of triangular Cycle wave IV, it is necessary to review the previous years, particularly the dynamic span of 1921 to 1929. Attention is therefore invited to component wave 5[3], shown in the accompanying graph of the Axe-Houghton Index, with this particular wave running from 1906 to 1929. The fifth or "e" wave, running from 1921 to the orthodox "extension" top of November 1928, was further subdivided as shown on page 38 of the Treatise. This pattern is referred to in my Treatise as a "half-moon." This movement was extremely

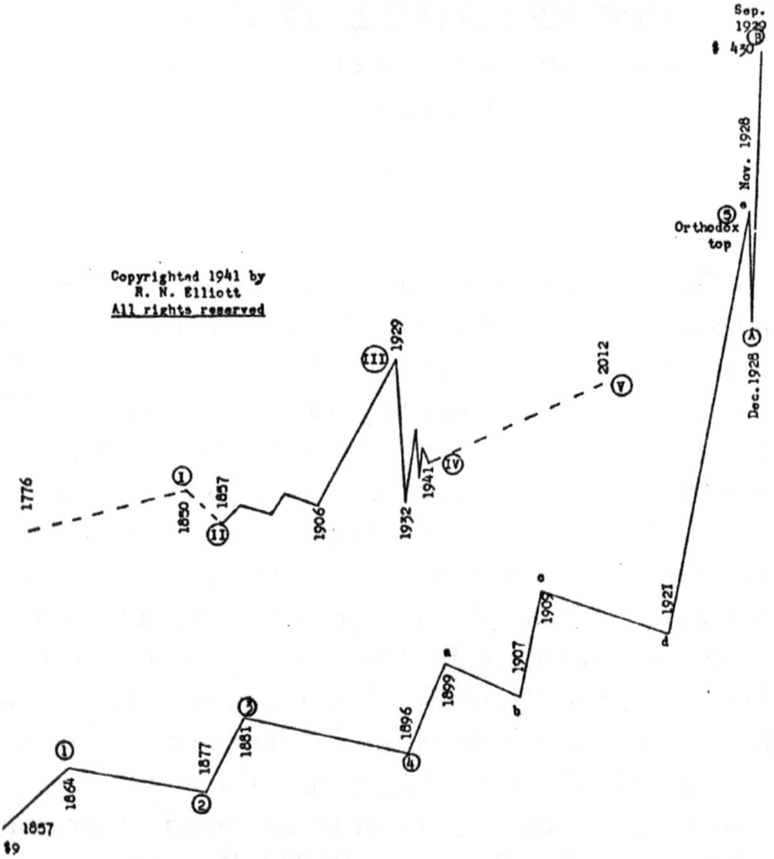

dynamic, accompanied by high speed, large volume and wild speculation. Furthermore, it was the culminating phase in the long span from 1857.

A cycle, such as that from 1857 to 1929 and containing such a frenzied movement as that from 1921 to 1929, necessarily requires an extensive correction, not only from the standpoint of price change but also in breadth of area or duration. High speed movements in one direction always generate proportionally high speed in the ensuing movement in the opposite direction.[4] The momentum carries over, in corrections, into the subsequent swings. Similarly, the extent, duration

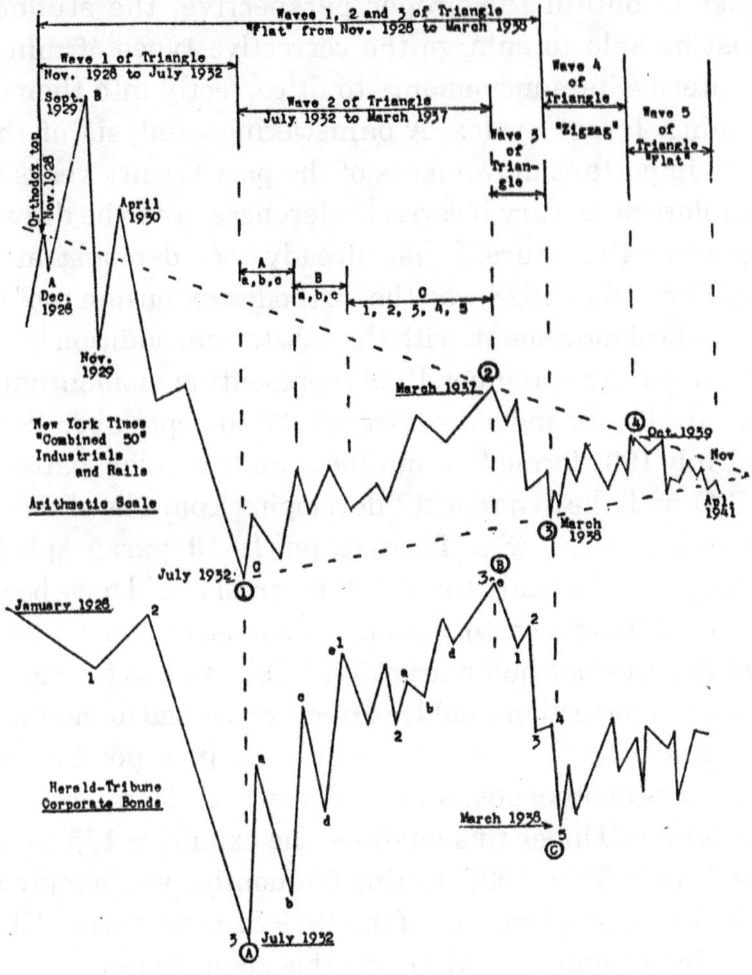

and volume characteristics are relative, cycle by cycle. In summation, the proportional arrangement of the necessarily extensive correction of the 1857-1929 wave called for shorter and shorter movements, together with decreasing speed and volume. Nature's inexorable law of proportion accounts for the recurrent 0.618 ratio of swing by swing comparison.

The Wave Principle is also proportional as regards both primary movements and corrective patterns. In order to obtain the proper perspective, the student must be able to enlarge the corrective types of minor or intermediate movements to fit correctly into themes of much larger cycles. A painstaking analysis of the more important movements of the past twenty years is therefore necessary if correct inferences are to be drawn regarding the future. It has already been demonstrated that November 1928 was the "orthodox extension top" of the cyclical movement, with the substantial addition from that point to September 1929 representing momentum.[5] Technically, the movement from 1928 to September 1929 and July 1932 formed the outline of an "irregular" pattern A-B-C, with the dynamic "C" developing from a level above the orthodox top. (See Treatise, pp. 18-19, paragraph 1, first figure.) Normally, this A-B-C reversal would have been the end of the cyclical correction, but it must be remembered that the previous bull market 1921-1929 was so extensive that a full correction would also require a broad foundation of years before the market would be in a position to commence another sustained "bull market" of large cyclical proportions. Under this analysis, the extensive 155-point rise from 1932 to 1937, lasting 55 months, was simply a technical "first" correction of the 1929-32 bear market. The following explanation will make this point clearer.

The whole movement (or movements) since 1928 (and also from April 1930) form a tremendous triangle, and this triangle is regarded as Cycle IV of an order dating back to as early as 1776.[6] The movement from November 1928 to March 1938 is regarded as a "flat" (3 down, 3 up, and 5 down), forming triangle waves ①, ② and ③.[7] Triangle wave ① ran from 1928 to July, 1932 in three huge component waves, with the third and most important wave starting from September 1929. (In the ratio triangle[8], the first waves runs downward from April 1930 to July 1932).

Triangle wave ② continued from July 1932 to March 1937, consisting of three waves instead of five. The first of these three waves was a "zigzag" (5 up, 3 down, and 5 up) and formed waves "a", "b" and "c" of "A" (see graph), running from July 1932 to July 1933. Wave "B" was a "flat," lasting from July 1933 to July 1934. Wave "C" was composed of five waves, July 1934 to March 1937. As thus analyzed, the movement from 1932 to 1937 was an upward "flat,"[9] instead of a normal bull market. *This is the only type of pattern that lends itself to two opposing interpretations.*[10] To properly visualize this description, turn the chart, bottom to top and face to back, against a window pane. "Double retracement" of the 1921-1928 extension was completed March 10, 1937.[11] This feature is best observed by examination of the Dow Jones Industrial average, monthly range.

Triangle wave ③ ran from March 10, 1937, to March 31, 1938, and also formed wave "C" of the "flat" counting from November 1928.

This picture is confirmed by the corporate bond index, a graph of which is shown herewith. Since the Treatise was written, I discovered that corporate bonds (particularly second grade rails) exert a dominating influence over equities. This feature has been mentioned several times in advisory letters. The pattern of this index from January 1928 to March 1938 is the same as this new interpretation of the cyclical trend of the industrial averages between the same points, that is, 3 down to 1932, 3 up to March 1937 and 5 down to March 1938. The bond index movement from July 1932 to March 1937 is plainly an upward "zigzag," as no other construction is possible; both "zigzags" and "flats" are corrections.

In regard to the corporate bond index which includes second grade rail bonds, it should be noted that the Dow

Jones Rail stock average touched 138 in 1906, at which time the Dow Jones Industrial Average was only 103; the ratio was 132. From that year until 1940, the ratio declined continuously to 20, a relative loss of 85%, Rails against Industrials. The span from 1906 to 1940 was 34 years, a potent unit of time. The Herald-Tribune second grade rail bonds declined to an all-time low figure of 26 during 1940, but have recovered recently to 52, a 100% gain.

Triangle wave ④, from March 31, 1938, to October, 1939, is a simple upward "zigzag," indicating that the movement was corrective in nature.

Triangle wave ① commenced in October 1939. It has taken the form of a "flat," similar to the pattern from November 1928, to March 1938, except that it is much smaller in extent and duration because of its nearness to the apex of the cyclical triangle. The first wave of the "flat" ran from October 1939 to June 1940; the second wave was upward from June to November, 1940; the third and final wave of the "flat" started in November 1940, and five Minor waves downward to May 1941 have already registered, but it is possible that these "five Minor waves" may be only wave 1 of wave "c" of the "flat." This question should be settled very soon.

At any event, Triangle wave ⑤ is well advanced, and its termination, within or without the area of the triangle, should mark the final correction of the 13-year pattern of *defeatism.*[12] This termination will also mark the beginning of a new Cycle wave V (composed of a series of cycles of lesser degree), comparable in many respects with the long cycle from 1857 to 1929. Cycle V is not expected to culminate until about 2012.[13] (See dashed line in first graph.)

R.N. Elliott

FOOTNOTES

[1] This and Interpretive Letter 18 are written much less like Interpretive Letters than like Educational Bulletins. They were simply notated "I L 17" and "I L 18" off to the side of the first page as if in afterthought, rather than the usual "Interpretive Letter No....." Since Educational Bulletins D through M are missing from the record, these labels cast some doubt as to whether they were sent only as Interpretive Letters or were used for the Educational Service as well. It is probable that Elliott wrote a flurry of articles in a short period of time and split them between the services. In fact, the letter entitled "Market Apathy - Cause and Termination," was written just prior to this one and sent unmarked. It is included in the "Educational Bulletins" section of this book.

[2] A remarkable conclusion, fully supported by the discovery of additional data. See Educational Bulletin O, the presentation in the Elliott Wave Principle, and Footnotes 26 and 52 in the "Nature's Law" section of The Major Works of R. N. Elliott.

[3] Labeled "e" on the chart and ending actually in 1928.

[4] While common in commodity prices, such behavior is rarely true in the stock market. In fact, the opposite often occurs. See Footnote 4 of Interpretive Letter No. 25.

[5] It is more valid and useful to label the orthodox peak in September 1929.

[6] Good call. The record shows the low in 1784.

[7] The 1937-1938 decline is a clear five wave structure, which is why Elliott labels it as part of a flat. Even as part of a flat, however, it would include a tremendous failure, not very likely. As a wave of a triangle, it breaks the rule that triangle legs must be threes. The Fibonacci relationships in this period were so striking that Elliott concluded they must be part of a single wave pattern, when in fact they existed across several patterns and parts of patterns, as he had correctly concluded in Interpretive Letter No. 8 (see Footnote 2). A. Hamilton Bolton and Charles Collins agreed that Elliott's labeling of the 13-year triangle was technically incorrect. Nevertheless, the triangular nature of the entire period is clear, and is undeniably

the best interpretation in the "constant dollar Dow," i.e. the DJIA adjusted for inflation, which unquestionably forms a triangle from 1929 to 1949. Elliott has understood the essence of the period, but by forcing it into a wave structure that isn't there, he employs a great deal of convoluted reasoning and upsets his own initial observations, meticulously derived from empirical observation, with regard to the rules of the Wave Principle. Indeed, these rules hold beautifully true throughout the period when the orthodox bottom of wave (IV) is correctly labeled as occurring in July 1932. Further footnotes will keep comments about Elliott's triangle to a minimum, under the assumption that the reader understands the situation.

[8] He means the triangle that produces Fibonacci relationships between the swings.

[9] This interpretation turns a five wave bull market into a "flat." It is a fine five wave bull market, but a horrendous flat correction, since wave B does not come anywhere near the start of the correction and wave C goes far beyond the end of wave A.

[10] The discussion under "The Right Look" in Elliott Wave Principle challenges and eliminates this contention.

[11] This rally does not fully retrace the 1921-1928 bull market. Elliott's concept here, if you take the time to study it, forces a clear guideline which is false into a highly complex one which is dubious at best.

[12] While the upcoming 1942 low is technically not the termination of a triangle, Elliott's conclusion is precisely correct and insightfully characterized.

[13] This estimate is based merely on an equivalent length to the 1857-1928 (orthodox top) advance, as he states in Educational Bulletin "O." Ironically, however, thrusts, as he points out elsewhere, are normally short and sharp, so this time estimate appears too far into the future given his triangle interpretation. Even forgetting the triangle, fifth waves are usually shorter than thirds. Regardless of these technical points, his call for a multi-decade advance in the midst of the gloom of 1942 is stunning in its foresight.

INTERPRETIVE LETTER No. 18
Duration or Time Element
August 27, 1941

In the analytical discussion of "The Basis of the Wave Principle,"[1] the composition of the waves of varying degrees was shown to be identical with the numerical relationships of the units making up the Fibonacci Summation Series of Dynamic Symmetry. This series is repeated, as follows: 1, 2, 3, 5, 8, 13, 21, 34, 55, 89, 144, etc. These relationships are very useful in identifying and measuring every wave and the extent of each movement, and when used in conjunction with The Wave Principle are also useful in forecasting the duration of trends in the various periods of time (days, weeks, months or years). The time element as an independent device, however, continues to be baffling when attempts are made to apply any known rule of sequence to trend duration.

An example of the use of the time element in conjunction with The Wave Principle is given in the accompanying graph of *The New York Times* average of 50 Combined Stocks, arithmetic scale, from August 1921, to May 1941. The various wave reversal points in this twenty-year period are listed in Table A, while the duration between reversal points is set forth in Table B.[2]

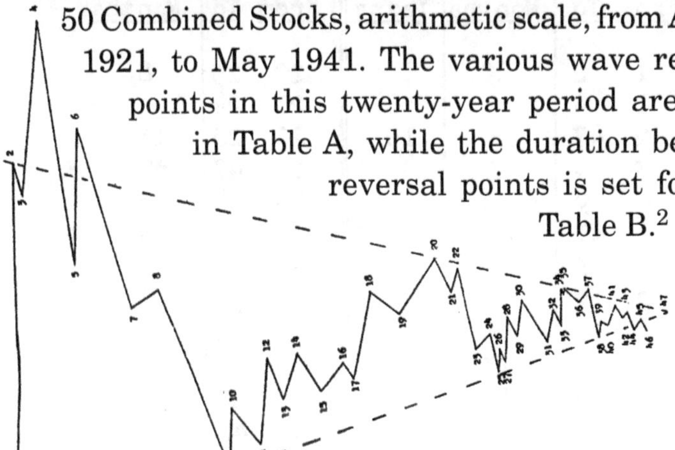

Table "A"
Numbers at reversal points

No.	Month	Year	No.	Month	Year
1	Aug.	1921	25	Mar.	1938
2	Nov.	28	26	Apl.	38
3	Dec.	28	27	May	38
4	Sep.	29	28	Jul.	38
5	Nov.	29	29	Sep.	38
6	Apl.	30	30	Nov.	38
9	Jul.	32	31	Apl.	39
10	Sep.	32	32	Aug.	39
11	Mar.	33	34	Sep.	39
12	Jul.	33	35	Oct.	39
13	Oct.	33	36	Jan.	40
14	Feb.	34	37	Apl.	40
15	Jul.	34	38	May	40
16	Jun.	35	39	Jun.	40
17	Mar.	35	40	Aug.	40
18	Nov.	35	41	Nov.	40
19	Apl.	36	42	Nov.	40
20	Mar.	37	43	Jan.	41
21	Jun.	37	44	Feb.	41
22	Aug.	37	45	Apl.	41
23	Oct.	37	46	May	41
24	Feb.	38	47	Oct.	41

Table "B"

Numbers		Duration		Numbers		Duration
From	To	Months	Years	From	To	Months
1	2	89		20	23	8
1	4		8	20	24	
2	47		13	20	25	13
3	4	8		20	47	55
4	9	34		23	24	5
4	47	144		25	30	8
5	6	5		30	31	5
9	12	13		31	34	5
9	20	55		35	36	3
12	15	13		35	47	
20	25	13		36	37	3
20	21	3		37	46	13
20	22	5		41	46	5

The time relationship can also be applied, in conjunction with wave analysis, to other indices, such as trends in corporate bonds in the graph below it. The five-wave bull market in long-term government bonds lasted 89 months, measured from January 1932, to June 1939. The numbers 13, 21 and 55 represent the number of months duration of waves, as indicated by arrows.

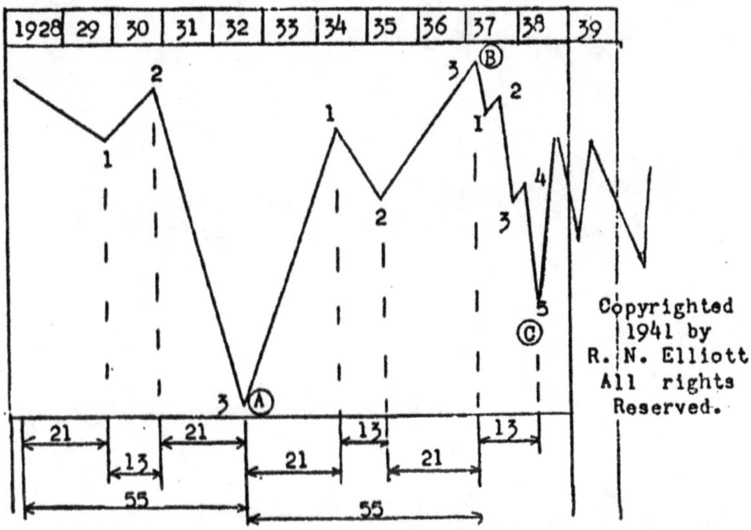

In studying the time element, it should be noted that a movement may start and end near the beginning, middle or end of a month, and for that reason the actual time elapsed, when measured by the day or week equivalent of the summation series of months, can terminate in a month next higher or lower than the series of months indicated. With The Wave Principle, the ratio of cyclical trends, the relative time for the movement, the mathematical nature of a triangle, and the Fibonacci Summation Series all stemming from the common source, the fact that all five measures point to an approaching culmination of a tremendous thirteen-year cyclical correction is extraordinary.

FOOTNOTES

[1] See Educational Bulletins.

[2] This is one of Elliott's great discoveries. I agree with both Elliott (see Interpretive Letter No. 21, Footnote 4) and Hamilton Bolton that while these time lengths do not occur in the market always and precisely, their occurrence is frequent enough to be well beyond coincidence.

INTERPRETIVE LETTER No. 19

A Novel Index

September 24, 1941

The graph below is an index of the ratio of yield of High Grade Bonds to that of Common Stocks. This pattern, complete in every detail, including the channel of wave Ⓒ, is a "zigzag" correction from August 1929 to April 1941.

This clear picture confirms the analysis of Interpretive Letter No. 17. (See "zigzag" pattern in Treatise, page 17, first diagram.)

R.N. Elliott

Duration:

Wave Ⓐ : 34 months	Numbers of
Wave Ⓑ : 13 months	Summation
Wave Ⓒ : 8 years	Series

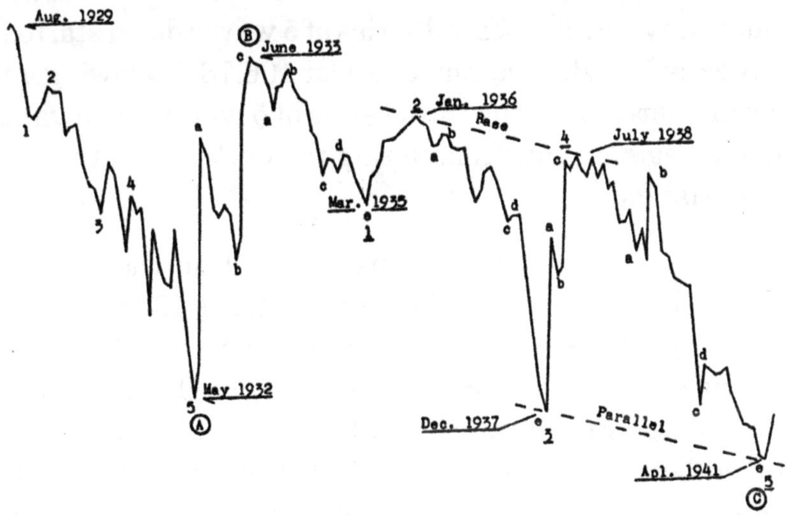

INTERPRETIVE LETTER No. 20

November 1940 - December 10, 1941

Three diagrams are shown in paragraph 1, page 17 of the Treatise. Attention is invited to diagrams "B" and "C". Wave "C" of diagram "B" is composed of *one* series of 5 waves, whereas wave "C" of diagram "C" is composed of *three* series of 5 waves each.

Interpretive Letter No. 17 described the 13-year triangle from November 1928 to May 1, 1941. Part of the text on page 3 is quoted herewith:

> "The third and final wave of the 'flat' started November 1940, and five Minor waves downward to May 1941 have already registered, but it is possible that these 'five Minor waves' may be only wave 1 of wave 'C' of the 'flat,' At any event, triangle wave 5 is well advanced, and its termination, within or without the area of the triangle, should mark the final correction of the 13-year triangle."

Graph **1** on the opposite page shows the D-J Industrial Average, weekly range, from November 1940 to December 10, 1941. The first series of 5 waves down ended May 1st. The second series of 5 waves down started July 28 and ended December 10, at 106.78. Following an upward correction, the third series of 5 waves downward should register, thus completing the decline and the 13-year triangle.[1]

Three triangles have registered within the big triangle. The first occurred between October 19, 1937 and February 23, 1938, as shown on pages 47 and 48 of the Treatise. The second occurred September-October 1939, as exhibited in Interpretive Letter No. 10. The third occurred between July 9 and 17, 1941 and forms the 4th Minute of the 5th Minor shown in graph **2** on the opposite page. None of these has been penetrated, and it is not known how much time must elapse before penetration is possible, as the daily range of stocks is not available, previous to 1928, for research. The current position of the market (December 15) lies between the first and third triangles above described.

Graph **3** demonstrates the divergence of the D J Industrial average and the Federal Reserve Production Index. Investors who are unfamiliar with triangles and

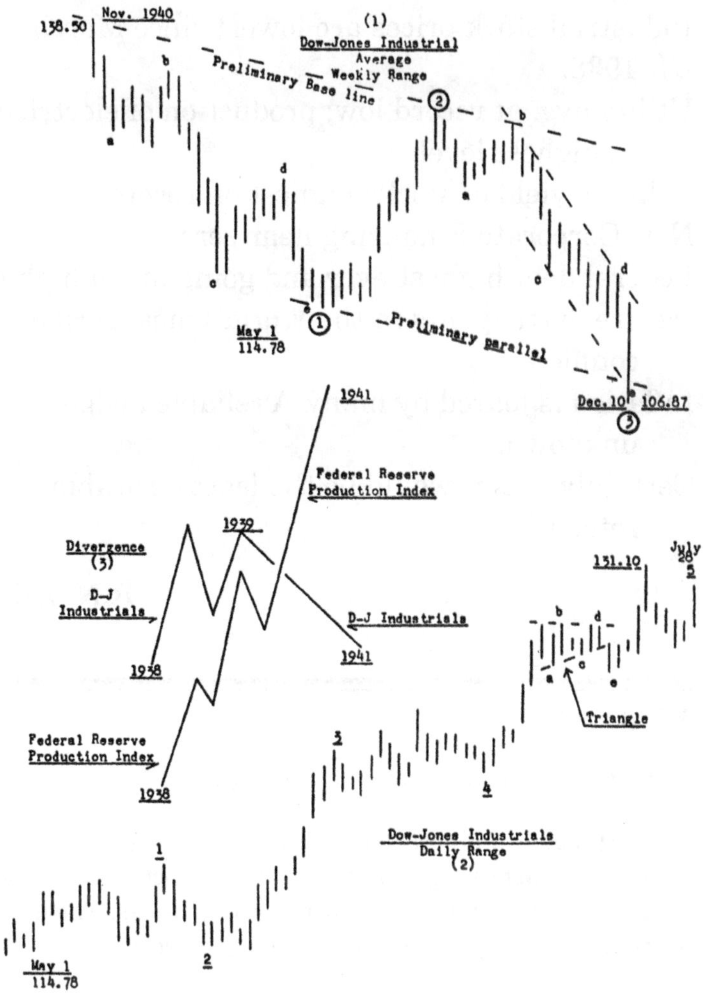

were guided by the Production Index suffered severe losses which they found expedient to register by tax-selling recently on account of high taxes, both present and prospective. This selling created additional downward pressure with the result that, on a comparative yield basis, stocks are cheaper today than they were in July 1932, as is graphically demonstrated in Interpretive Letter No. 19.

Production recently completed 5 major waves upward.
Industrial stock prices are lowest since March 1938.
Utility avg. at record low; production of electricity at highest level.
Relative yield of stocks highest on record.
New Corporate Financing near zero.
Federal debt highest ever and going much higher.
We are participants in the World's most serious conflict.
Inflation is feared by many. A reliable hedge is unknown.
Certainly "cash" would be the least desirable refuge.[2]

R.N. Elliott

FOOTNOTES

[1] Elliott is right; the decline is not yet over.

[2] Elliott makes an increasingly compelling case for a developing major long term buying opportunity in the stock market and an upcoming multi-decade, many-multiple rise in prices. The quarter century that followed proved him gloriously correct.

INTERPRETIVE LETTER No. 21[1]

Attention is invited to Interpretive Letter No. 17 and in particular to the graph showing the movement from October 1939, at which point the end of wave (4) is shown. Please also review the last two paragraphs of text in that letter. On the next page of the present Letter will be found four graphs, **W**, **X**, **Y** and **Z**, all of which describe the Dow Jones Industrial Average.

Graph **W** is an outline of the movement from October 1939 to March 12, 1942. This is the 5th and last wave of the 13-year Triangle,[2] but is not yet completed. For pattern, see Treatise, page 17, paragraph 1, figure C.

Graph ***X*** shows the weekly range from November 1940, which details wave Ⓒ of graph **W** mentioned in the preceding paragraph. Wave Ⓒ of a flat should be composed of 5 waves. The 5th wave is incomplete.

Graph ***Y*** is an outline of graph **X**. Note the dashed Base Line drawn against the ends of waves 2 and 4, and the Parallel Line drawn against the end of wave 3. Wave 5 (incomplete) rests on the Parallel Line. Ordinarily, this would confirm the termination of the "flat" of graph **W**.

Graph **Z** shows the daily range of wave 4 (December 10 to January 6). Its pattern is an "irregular flat" inverted. (See last figure on page 16 of the Treatise.) Turn the page upside down and front to back.

Wave 4 in graph **X** (December 10 to January 6, 1942) is inconspicuous and relatively small in amplitude and duration. Compare it with wave 2 (May-July, 1941). The reason for this disparity is that during December 1941 "tax selling" was unusually heavy. This caused a "throw-over" at the end of wave 3 (December 10), thus providing a depressed base for wave 4. Moreover, its duration was only one month, whereas wave 2 (May-July, 1941) consumed 3 months. If wave 4 had not been distorted by tax selling, wave 5 would have started about ten points higher and its first leg would have ended far above the parallel line.

The behavior of the Industrial Average following March 12, 1942 is bearish, which confirms lower prices.[3]

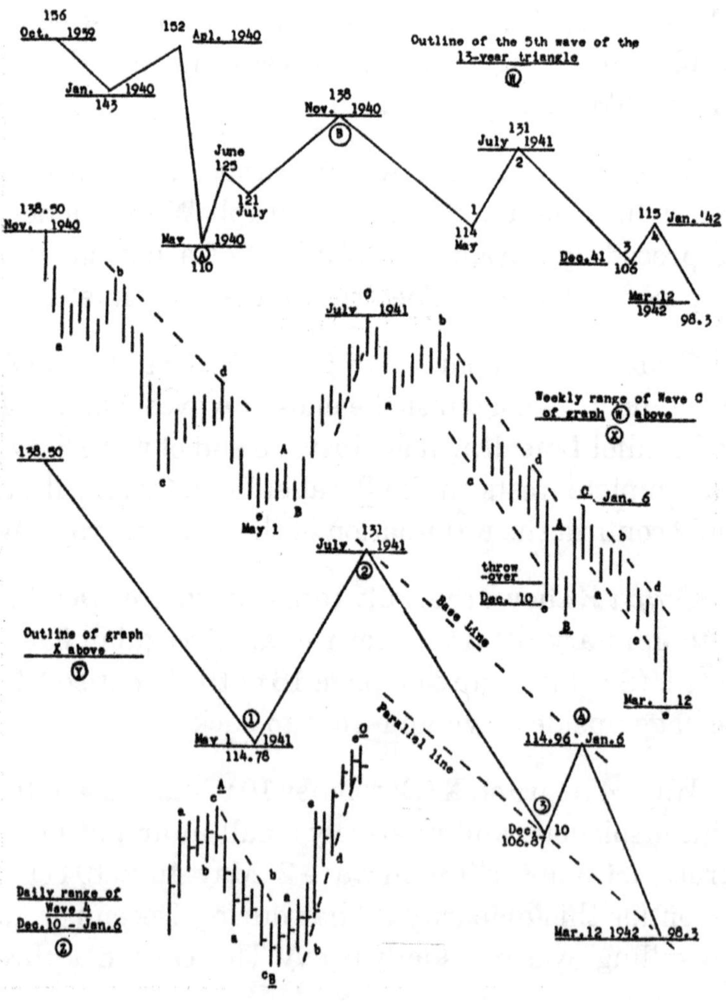

The Fibonacci Summation Series is the basis of The Wave Principle. The Time Element is based on the same Series but has its limitations and can be used only as an adjunct of The Wave Principle.[4] An excellent opportunity is presented to utilize the Time Element. For convenient reference, the numbers of the Summation Series are repeated herewith: 3 - 5 - 8 - 13 - 21 - 34, etc. The Time Element was demonstrated in Interpretive Letter No. 18; I recommend that you review same.

The next graph shows the elapsed time in months, both actual and estimated. Waves Ⓐ and Ⓑ from October 1939 to November 1940 consumed 13 months. From November 1940 to March 1942 only 16 months elapsed, whereas in the Summation Series, the next number above 13 is 21. November 1940 plus 21 months equals August 1942. October 1939 plus 34 months equals the same month of August. August is therefore the indicated termination of wave Ⓒ of the flat, the 13-year Triangle and the extreme low point. Interpretive Letter No. 18 demonstrates that one month's tolerance is customary.[5]

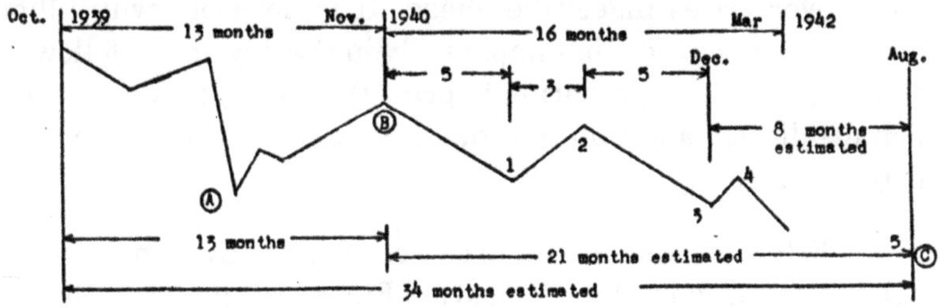

The component units of 21 are 5, 3, 5, 3 and 5. Waves 1, 2 and 3 consumed 5, 3 and 5 months respectively, total 13 months, to December 1941. December 1941 plus 8 months equal August.

If all 5 waves downward from January 1942 are approximately of the same duration as waves 1 and 2, the result would be as follows:

Wave 1	January and February
Wave 2	March
Wave 3	April and May,
Wave 4	June,
Wave 5	July and August.

Total 8 months.

R.N. Elliott

FOOTNOTES

[1] The date was left off of this letter, but based upon the charts, it appears to have been published on March 13, 1942.

[2] In anything but an expanding triangle, wave e, the final wave, should not exceed the termination point of wave c. The drop in 1942 to below the 1938 low was yet another indication that Elliott's triangle concept was invalid. See chart, Interpretive Letter No. 25.

[3] Lower prices indeed lie ahead. It is not clear why Elliott came to this conclusion, but apparently in the day or two following March 12, as he was preparing to print this issue, action occurred which disallowed a low on that date, so he added this sentence, a timely warning.

[4] Elliott is entirely correct in this conclusion. Even today, many people program computers to provide Fibonacci time lengths as a sole means of analysis, to little avail.

[5] The low occured in April. However, the low for wave two of the new bull market (and for volume; see Footnote 1 of Interpretive Letter No. 22) occurred in August.

INTERPRETIVE LETTER No. 22
Volume
June 22, 1942

The Wave Principle is applicable to all three factors of the stock market: Price Index, Time Element and Volume. My Treatise covers the Price Index and briefly mentions volume on page 24. The Time Element is discussed in Interpretive Letters Nos. 18 and 21.

Volume behavior is disclosed on the next page. All four graphs show the Average Daily Volume from 1878 to June 13, 1942. Each graph covers different time periods.

*Graph **1*** shows the Daily Volume from 1878 to 1941. Note the 5 waves up to 1929.

*Graph **2*** is a 3-year moving average from 1929 to 1941 and clarifies the wave motion of this period in graph **1**. Wave "C" shows a continuous decline.

*Graph **3*** is a detail of Wave "C" of graph **2**. It is a 3-months moving average from 1937 to May 1942. Note the 5 subdivisions, a, b, c, d and e, of waves ① and ③.

*Graph **4*** is a detail of the last wave of graph 3 ("e" of ③), January 10 to June 13, 1942. (By weeks, not a moving average.)

Wave "C" of graph **2** should have 5 waves down. Only waves 1, 2 and 3 have registered thus far, as per graph **3**. In a downward trend, corrective waves 2 and 4 register an increase in volume.

Presumably wave ④ (an increase in volume) will cover two periods of the Price Index:

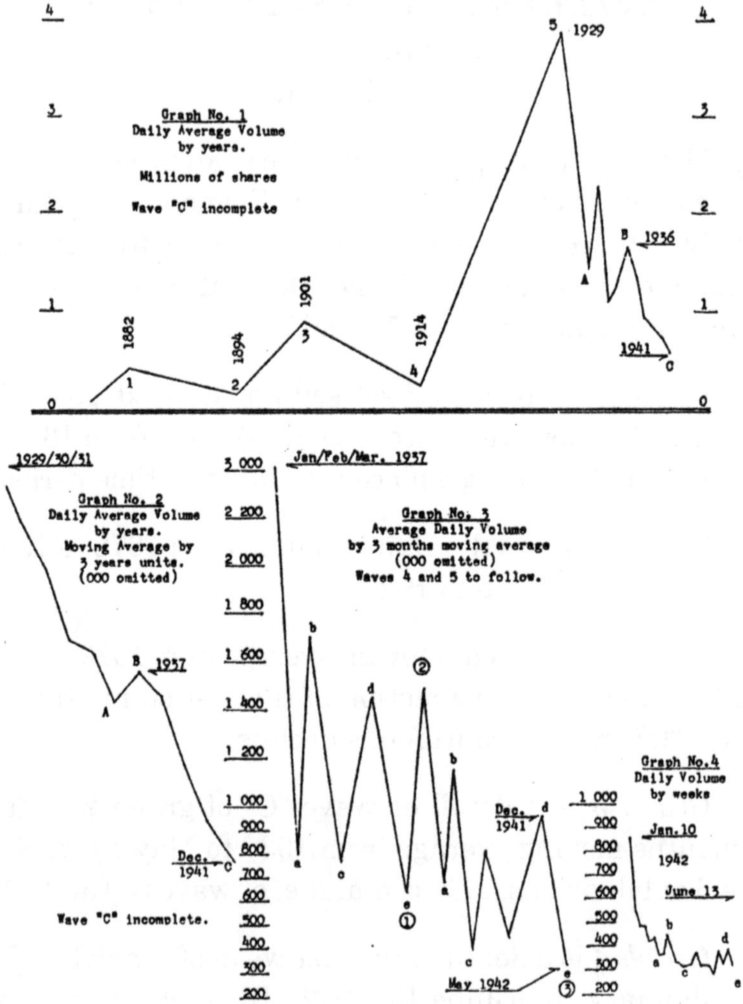

a. the final decline and
b. the first advance of the approaching bull market.

Wave 5, being a decrease in volume, will probably cover the period of the first correction of the approaching bull market.[1] This practice is frequent but not invariable.[2] Graphs of the Dow Jones averages show the extreme low of price during March, and of volume during June 1938.

Duration and Volume are useful adjuncts to The Wave Principle.

R.N. Elliott

P.S. The R-M Series by Mr. Martin[3] is creating favorable comment.

One subscriber says that The Wave Principle is "becoming an exact science." May I have your impressions?

FOOTNOTES

[1] This remarkable forecast came to pass. Volume picked up briefly in early July in the first wave of the new bull market, then in early August during wave two it slackened to the lowest point of the year on six-day moving average basis (stocks traded for two hours on Saturday then).

[2] This is a very useful observation. If, after a long decline, volume drops to new lows but price does not, conditions are in place for a powerful third wave to the upside.

[3] This note refers to Richard Martin, a former student of Elliott's whom he licensed to practice the Wave Principle professionally (for more details, see the biography in *R.N. Elliott's Masterworks*.

INTERPRETIVE LETTER No. 23
Long Range Behavior of Rails
October 26, 1942

Below will be found a table of ratios between the Rails and Industrials on several dates commencing with January 1906, when the Rails registered an important top, and a graph of these ratios.

	Industrials	*Rails*	*Ratio*
January, 1906	103.00	138.36	134.2
September, 1929	381.17	189.11	49.6
July, 1932	41.22	13.25	32.0
March, 1937	195.00	64.46	33.0
June 10, 1940	110.84	22.79	20.2
October 2, 1942	110.85	28.51	25.7

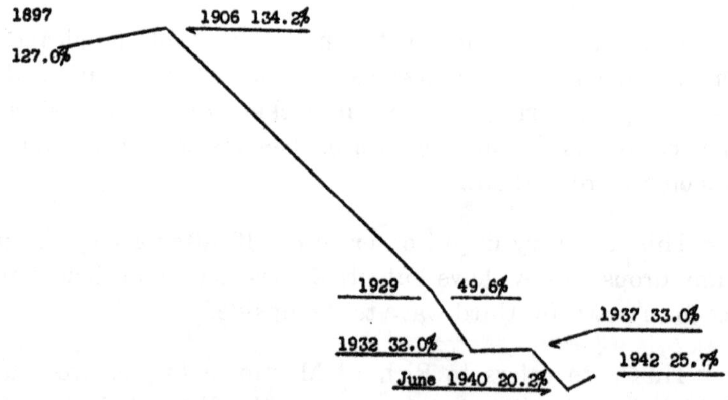

In 1906, the Hepburn Act empowered the I.C.C. to control the Railroads, which was the first application of bureaucratic regulation.[1] In 1914 (8 years later), the Panama Canal was opened for traffic and inaugurated severe competition with the Railroads (more especially the transcontinental lines), which the present war has suspended.

In June 1940 (34 years after 1906), the Rails registered a bottom and for the first time since 1906, the ratio reversed. The pattern above the low of 1940 extended, confirming major reversal.[2] At that time, one third of the Rail mileage was in receivership and another third on the borderline.

From 1906 to 1940, the Rail Index was usually first to register a top and last to confirm a bottom. This feature has reversed since 1940 and may continue its present practice for a considerable period of time.[3]

Rail Bonds dominate the Corporate Bond Index, which likewise extended upward from June 1940, and is now above its 1941 top.

R.N. Elliott

FOOTNOTES

[1] Congress, after years of providing inordinate support and monopoly rights to developers of the railroad industry, destroyed the rail industry in the United States with the stroke of a pen.

[2] Correct. That low was never broken.

[3] Elliott's notation that 1906 to 1940 was 34 years suggests that the rails should lead for about 55 years, until 1995. Indeed, this situation has lasted all the way to September 1989. Action in the three years since then suggests that this tendency is in fact ending.

INTERPRETIVE LETTER No. 24
The 5th Wave of the 13-year Triangle1
December 4, 1942

As shown in Interpretive Letter No. 17, wave ④ of the large triangle ended October 1939. On the opposite page, graph **W** shows wave 5 to October 1942, lacking only the 5th wave of ©, which is tentatively indicated by a dashed line.[1] Theoretically, wave 5 of © should be approximately the same length and angle as wave 1 of ©. In the Treatise on page 17, paragraph 1, diagram C, is shown the pattern of this entire movement. Graph **Z** is a reproduction of the D-J Industrial average between July 1933 and July 1934. Graphs **W** and **Z** are "flats."

Graph **X** shows in detail waves 3 and 4 of graph **W**. Wave Ⓐ[2] from April 1942 to July 15 embraces 5 Minor waves. Wave Ⓑ from July 15 to September 16 represents a triangle. Wave © to October 13 was the usual thrust that follows triangles and marks the end of the movement from April 1942. This thrust extended and the extension was double-retraced between October 15 and November 9, as is customary.[3]

Between September 1941 and April 1942, all industrial averages are distorted in detail. In graph **X**, wave 3 embraces only 3 Minor waves, and wave 5 is composed of 7 waves of Minor degree.[4] The channel is far from perfect.

Graph **Y** shows perfect composition and channeling. Wave 3 is composed of 5 minor waves, "a" to "e". Likewise wave 5. Note the Base and Parallel lines of the channel, a perfect pattern.

Graph **Y**[5] is a new index and solves the problem. It also demonstrates that the popular averages are geared to peace conditions, and that the distortion of wave movements was due to shifting of industry from peace to war.

R.N. Elliott

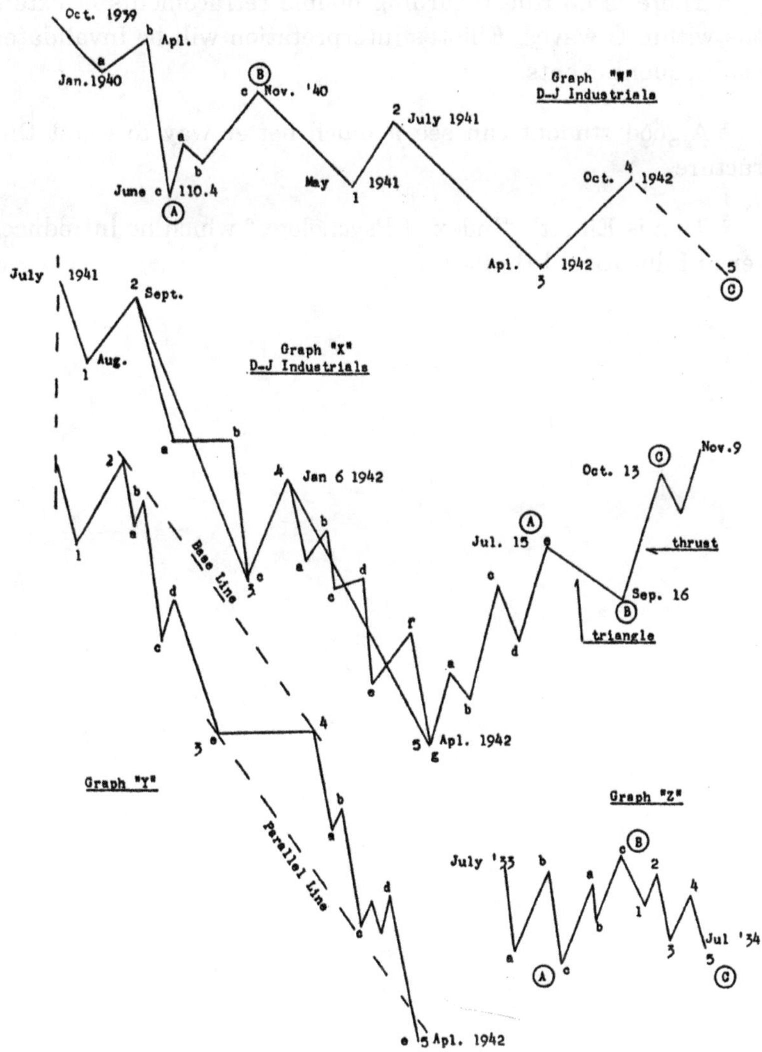

FOOTNOTES

[1] Elliott's interpretation in Interpretive Letter No. 21 was closer to the mark.

[2] Elliott had yet to adhere faithfully to a labeling method for specific degrees. He is using circled letters for the triangle legs as well as for their subwaves.

[3] There is no rule regarding double retracements of extensions within C waves. Elliott's interpretation will be invalidated by subsequent events.

[4] A good student can see a much better way to count this structure.

[5] This is Elliott's "Index of Psychology," which he introduces later in Educational Bulletin P.

INTERPRETIVE LETTER No. 25
The 13-year Triangle
December 15, 1942

The 13-year bear market was created by the following forces:

1. Transition, during some 60 years, from one-manfarms to extensive incorporated industrial development of a vast virgin territory blessed with enormous natural resources.
2. Consequent gigantic amplitude of the 1921-1928 wave.
3. Extension of same.
4. Double retracement of the extension, and
5. Time.

Note that politics, wars and current events are not mentioned.

The graph following and the diagrams below, copied from my Treatise, demonstrate that mass psychology observes definite patterns as described in my Treatise.

As will be noted by graphs on page 37,[1] the duration of bear markets is longer than that of bull markets.[2] The duration of the movement from 1921 to 1929 was 8 years, therefore the succeeding bear market should consume more time.[3] The next potent number is 13.

The triangle on page 22, pgf. 2,[1] diagram "B" is an outline of the entire period, 1921-1943. Note the triangle wave numbers at the bottom of the large graph.

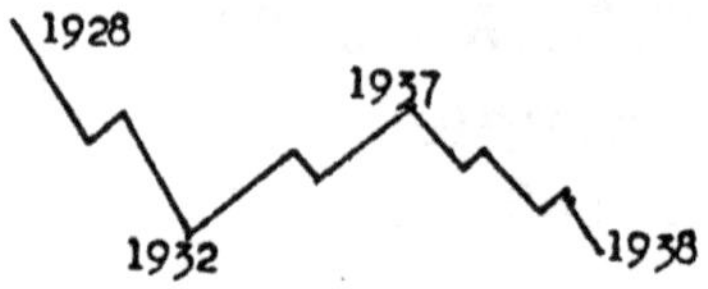

Waves 1, 2 and 3 of the triangle form a "flat" as shown on page 17, pgf. 1, diagram "B".

Triangle wave 4 is a "zigzag", inverted, as shown on page 17, pgf.1, diagram "A".

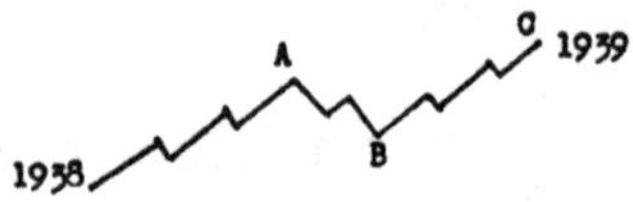

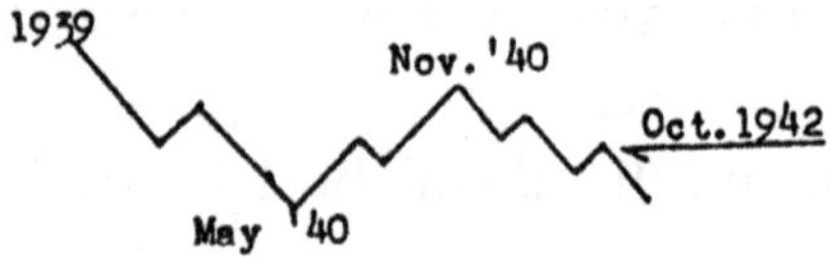

Triangle wave 5 is a "flat" as shown on page 17, pgf. 1, diagram "C".

Patterns described in the Treatise may appear in any degree.

All corrective patterns described in the Treatise apply to bull trends. For bear trends, corrective patterns must be inverted.

A rapid movement in one direction is always followed by a reverse movement of a slightly lesser speed.[4] Note the lesser speed of each successive triangular wave.[5]

Double retracement of the 1921-1928 extension was completed in March 1937. All minor extensions were double-retraced individually.

R.N. Elliott

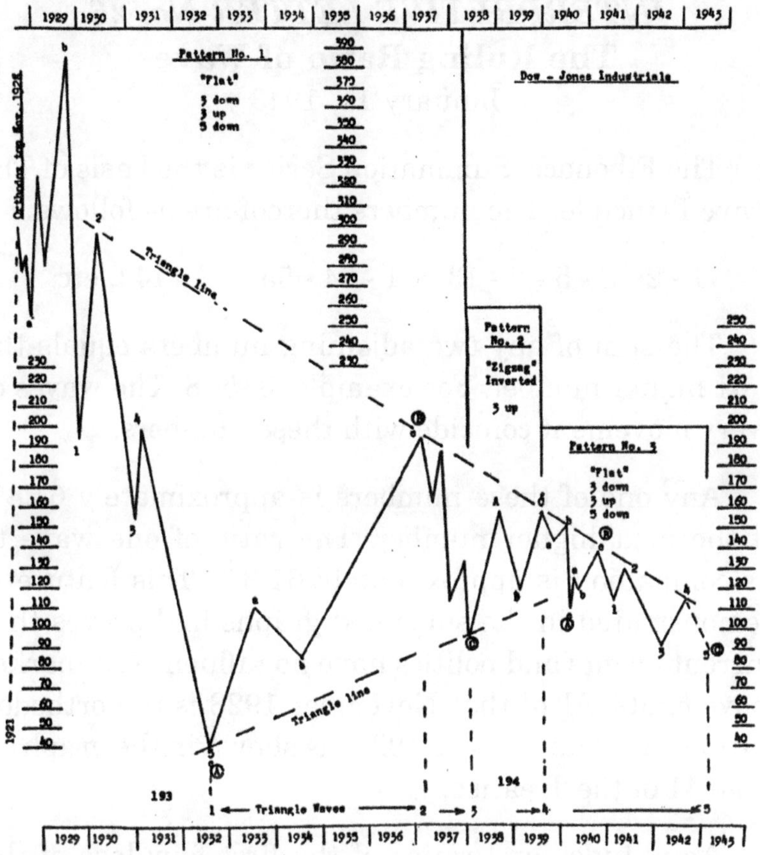

FOOTNOTES

[1] These various references are to his Treatise, "The Wave Principle."

[2] See Footnote 6 in Interpretive Letter No. 8.

[3] This bear market corrected the entire rise from 1857 to 1929, and was therefore clearly a shorter time.

[4] Elliott has revised his earlier comment in Interpretive Letter No. 17 (see Footnote 4 thereof).

[5] In most cases, "A" waves in triangles, and indeed in most corrections, are the most dramatic.

INTERPRETIVE LETTER No. 26
The Ruling Ratio of Waves
January 11, 1943

The Fibonacci Summation Series is the basis of The Wave Principle. The numbers thereof are as follows:

1 - 2 - 3 - 5 - 8 - 13 - 21 - 34 - 55 - 89 - 144, etc.

The sum of any two adjoining numbers equals the next higher number. For example: 3+5=8. The waves of every movement coincide with these numbers.

Any one of these numbers is approximately 61.8% of the next higher number. The ratio of one wave to its companion is approximately 61.8%. This feature is demonstrated in the subjoined graphs and proves that current events and politics have no influence on market movements. Also[1] that November 1928 is the orthodox top of the advance above 1921, as shown in the graph on page 41 of the Treatise.

Amplitudes and ratios of the first four legs of the triangle are shown below:

Wave	*Dates*		*Price*				
	From	*To*	*From*	*To*	*Pts*	*Ratio*	*Avg*
1	Nov '28	Jul '32	296.0	40.5	255.5		
2	Jul '32	Mar '37	40.5	196.0	155.5	155.5/255.5 = 60.9%	
3	Mar '37	Mar '38	196.0	97.0	99.0	99.0/155.5 = 63.6%	62%
4	Mar '38	Sep '39	97.0	158.0	61.0	61.0/99.0 = 61.6%	

As stated in the Treatise, the 5th leg of a triangle may not terminate within the triangular outline. However, it must be composed of 3 waves, the same as each of the other four legs. In the present instance, the 3 waves of

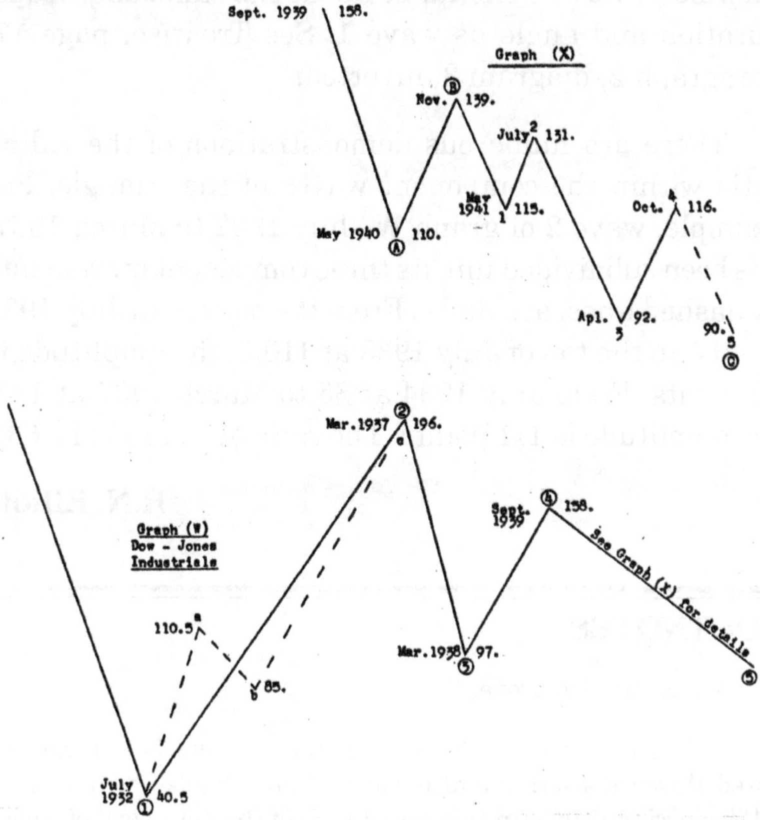

the 5th leg form a "flat" pattern as shown on page 17 of the Treatise, i.e., 3 waves down, 3 waves up and 5 waves down (A, B and C). The entire pattern of the "flat" is now complete, with the exception of the 5th wave of "C", as shown by a dashed line in graph X.

The details of the 5th leg of the triangle are shown in graph **X**. The component waves of this "flat" pattern also conform to the ruling ratio. Wave Ⓑ is about 61.8% of wave Ⓐ. In wave Ⓒ, wave 1 is 61.8% of wave 3. The orthodox top of wave 4 registered on October 13 at 116, 24 points above the April bottom, or 61.5% of wave 3.

Therefore, wave 5 should be about the same amplitude, duration and angle as wave 1. See Treatise, page 17, paragraph 2, diagram 3, inverted.

There are numerous demonstrations of the ruling ratio within the component waves of the triangle. For example, wave 2 of graph **W**, July 1932 to March 1937, has been subdivided into its three component movements by dashed lines, a, b and c. From the bottom in July 1932 at 40.5 to the top of July 1933 at 110.5, the amplitude is 70 points. From July 1934 at 85 to March 1937 at 196, the amplitude is 111 points. The ratio of 70 to 111 is .63.[2]

R.N. Elliott

FOOTNOTES

[1] I. e., "It also proves."

[2] Elliott's later observation (in Interpretive Letter No. 33, dated March 1945) that a fifth wave, when extended, will often be a Fibonacci multiple (in this case 1.618) of the net travel of waves 1 through 3 is also satisfied here, and more accurately reflects the better count.

INTERPRETIVE LETTER No. 27
Primary No. 1, 1942 - 1943[1]

Interpretive Letter No. 25 indicated 5 Intermediate waves downward from October 1942 to approximately 90 (D-J Industrials), which would have completed the pattern of the 13-year bear-market triangle. The cause of incompletion is fully explained in Bulletin "P",[2] entitled "Index of Psychology."[3]

Graph **X** on the next page is the weekly range of the D-J Industrials from April 1942 to April 1943, scale 8 points to the inch.[4] This movement is Primary wave 1 of a new bull market[5] and is composed of 5 Intermediate waves as shown by their respective numbers.[6] Note the dashed channel lines. Its pattern is similar to the 3rd diagram, paragraph 3, page 17 of the Treatise.

Intermediate wave 1 from April 28 to July 9, 1942 is composed of 5 Minor waves, as will be noted.

Intermediate wave 2 from July 9 to September 11, 1942 is a triangle.

Intermediate wave 3 from September 11 to October 13, 1942 is the usual "thrust" that follows a triangle. It is composed of 9 Minors, visible in the daily range (extension).

Intermediate wave 4 from October 13 to November 24, 1942 is an "*irregular flat*," 3 down, 3 up and 5 down. See Treatise, page 16, last diagram.

Intermediate wave 5 from November 24, 1942 to April 6, 1943 is longer than Intermediate waves 1 and 3 combined. (See Treatise, page 17, paragraph 2, diagram No. 3.) Minor wave 3 extended.

Graph **Y** shows the daily range of Intermediate wave 5, scale 4 points to the inch. Minor waves 1 to 5 are so marked. *A "simple" corrective is a 3 wave movement of the smallest pattern. A "complex" corrective is an enlarged pattern and is usually composed of 7 wavelets which are called "double 3s", as described in previous letters. These two types alternate, that is, if a "simple" appears as wave 2, a "complex" will appear as wave 4, and vice versa. Whenever an upward movement is composed of 3 waves, it is part of a "correction."*[7] In the present instance, Minor wave 2 is a "simple" and Minor wave 4 is "complex."

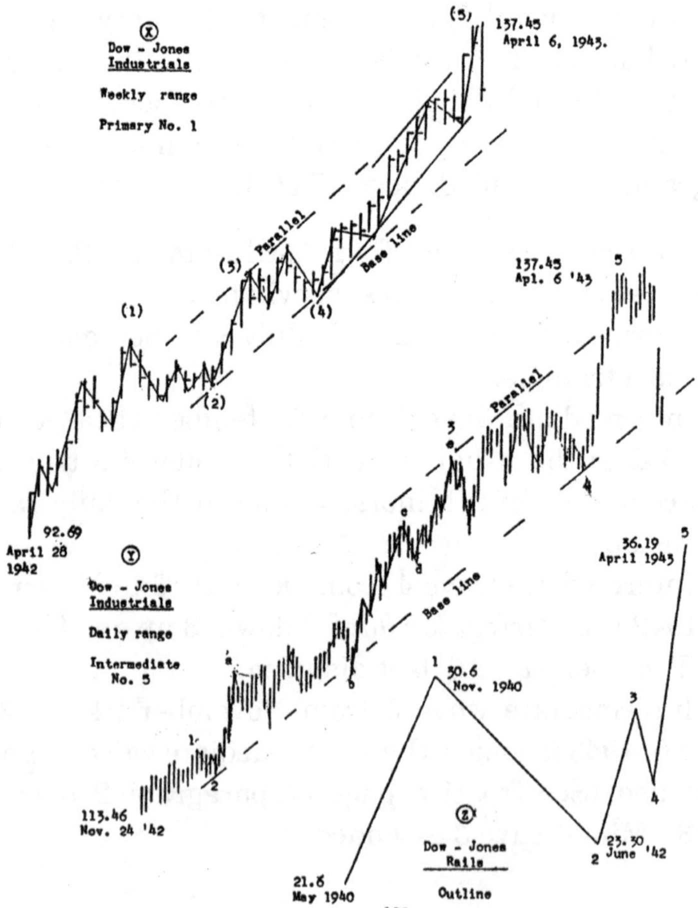

198

Minor wave 3 extended and is marked by the letters a, b, c, d and e. Minute wave "b" is "complex" and Minute wave "d" is "simple." Note that waves a, c and e are composed of 5 Minuette waves each. See Treatise, page 17, paragraph 2, diagram 3.

Graph **Z**, Dow Jones Rails, is shown to call attention to the fact that this average has developed only 3 waves upward from June 1942. Examine carefully Interpretive Letter No. 23. The movement from May to November 1940 was composed of 5 waves and extended, thus indicating that May 1940 might have been bottom, as it has since proved to be. Two years elapsed between the beginning of wave 1 and the end of wave 2.

Composite corporate bonds developed nearly the same pattern as the rails.

London Industrials registered bottom on June 1940. From that date to January 19, 1943, 5 Intermediate waves have registered. Since January 19, this index is forming Primary wave 2, sidewise within a range of 2 points.

R.N. Elliott

FOOTNOTES

[1] This letter's publication date appears to be April 7, 1943.

[2] I.e., Educational Bulletin P.

[3] See Footnote 6 of Educational Bulletin P.

[4] Scale not valid for this book.

[5] Despite previous errors, Elliott adjusts quickly and is absolutely correct that a new bull market has begun.

[6] This labeling places a triangle in the wave (2) position. His Financial World articles in 1939 address the idea that triangles occur only in the fourth wave position. He formalized this idea as a guideline in Educational Bulletin "O" less than six months prior to this issue. Nonetheless, he ignores the guideline in labeling this chart. The short third wave, like so many others in previous letters, also breaks a rule he formulated later (see Footnote 8, of Interpretive Letter No. 1 and Footnote 1 of Interpretive Letter No. 28).

[7] Elliott's first reference to what would later become the Rule of Alternation appeared in "The Wave Principle." He ignored the idea in many Interpretive Letters. In fact, this is the first reference to it in any of his periodicals. He described the concept further in Educational Bulletins **W** and **ZA**.

INTERPRETIVE LETTER No. 28

January 10, 1944

Interpretive Letter No. 27 showed 5 Intermediate waves upward from April 1942 to April 6, 1943, an outline of which is shown in graph **X** on the next page. Following a correction of Minor degree from April 6 to 13, 1943, the Industrial average advanced in 5 Minor waves, equivalent to one Intermediate wave, to July 15 at 146.41.[1] The fact that this 7th wave was composed of 5 Minor waves up and that the Base Line had not yet been penetrated suggested the possibility that inflation had started. For a complete discussion of inflationary characteristics, please review the bulletin of September 20, 1943, entitled "Inflation."[2]

On July 25, 1943, Sunday, the unexpected happened: Mussolini was removed after 21 years of dictatorship. Our Industrial average immediately penetrated the Base Line (see graph) and declined to 133.87 on August 2, thereby reversing public war psychology and the inflationary aspects.

The correction thus far (July-November 1943) is "simple." I have frequently mentioned that corrective waves 2 and 4 (of any degree) alternate in character. If wave 2 is "simple," then wave 4 will be "complex," and vice versa. Therefore, we do not know beforehand if wave 2 will be a "simple" or "complex" correction. A "simple" correction is the minimum requirement, i.e., one series of 3 waves. A "complex" is an enlargement thereof, in essence a "double 3," so to speak. In any event, whether simple or complex, the Base Line must be penetrated, except in the event of inflation. In other words, when a correction does not penetrate the Base Line, inflation is indicated. In the present instance, corrective Primary wave 2 of the Industrial average penetrated its Base Line in July 1943, but the Rails barely touched their Base Line on November 30, 1943 at 31.42. My Psychology Index barely penetrated its Base Line the week of November 27, 1943.

As will be noted in graph **X**, wave e of corrective wave Ⓒ declined to 128.94 on November 30. This 5th wave was very short, relatively.[3] Note that it did not reach the Parallel Line of the small channel. If it had done so, the low point would have reached 124 in December 1943, as forecast in "Confidential Letters."[4] However, this circumstance is of little importance. The all important feature now is, will the current rally develop 5 waves or only 3 Minor waves upward? It is now (January 8) in its 3rd Minor wave (see graph **X**). If only 3 Minor waves register, then the Bull Market *completed* its course on July 15, 1943, and lower prices will be seen. If 5 Minor waves upward develop, then the Bull Market has not terminated, and higher prices will register. From statistical and political angles, there is much evidence, both pro and con.

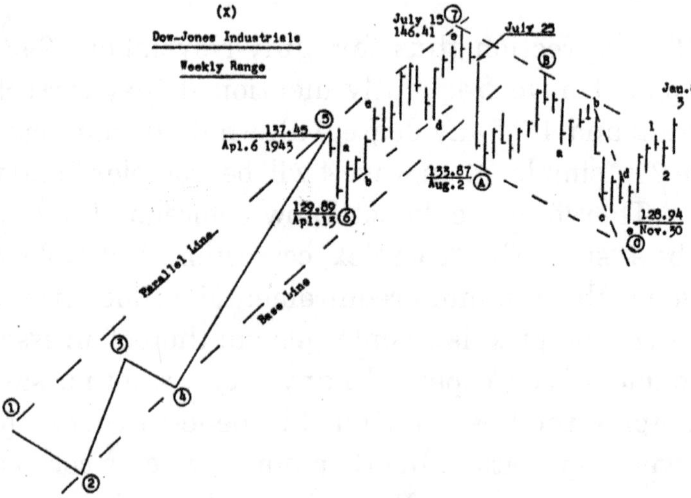

(Y)

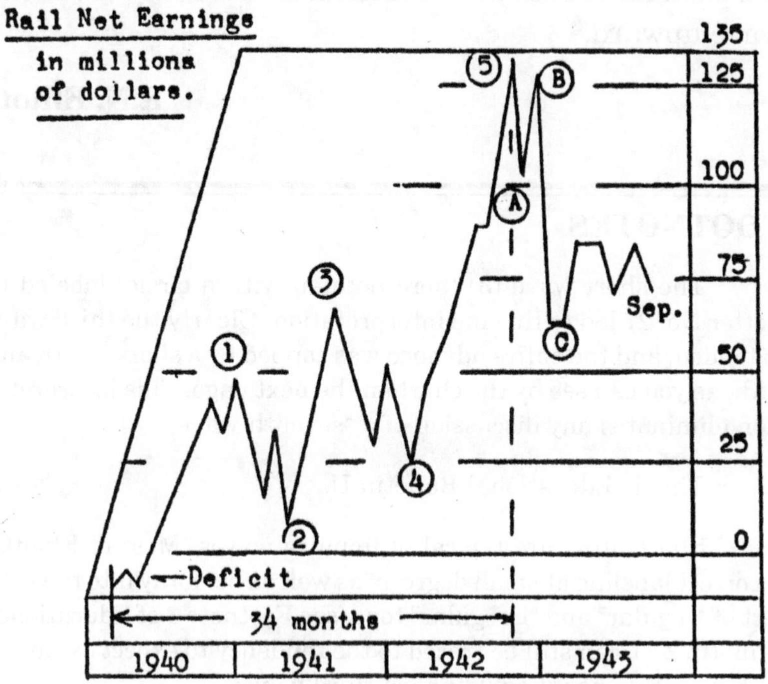

From Herald-Tribune Nov. 28, 1943.

Graph **Y** above shows Net Earnings of Class 1 railroads from January 1940 to September 1943. Note the 5 major waves upward for 34 months from January 1940 to October 1942. The Price average for the Rails registered 5 waves upward from May 1940 to 1943. See Interpretive Letter No. 27.

The contents of this Letter demonstrate why it has not been possible of late to issue Interpretive Letters more frequently.

From the Time angle, I estimate that the war will end during the last quarter of 1944.[5] *The New York Times* of January 7, 1944, page 8, published a graph of "Lend

Lease," which clearly indicated that as of October 1943, the peak had about been reached, lacking only one small wave upward.

R.N. Elliott

FOOTNOTES

[1] The short wave (3) (here notated with a circle) labeled in Letter No. 27 led to this misinterpretation. Clearly the third wave extended, and the entire advance was capped by a short fourth and fifth, as you can see by the chart on the next page. This interpretation eliminates any discussion of a "seventh wave."

[2] This is Educational Bulletin U.

[3] Short fifths are typical of impulse waves. Most of Elliott's incorrect labeling at small degrees, as well as his foray into the subject of "regular" and "irregular" tops (see Footnote 3 of Educational Bulletin ZA), can still be traced to the tendency to expect extended fifth waves rather than extended third waves.

[4] A Forecast Letter, not available.

[5] Certainly a terrific "call," considering that the war could have gone on for years.

INTERPRETIVE LETTER No. 29[1]

An examination of the Rail Index is interesting, informative and profitable.

Transportation is the most important human factor in our economy because of the great distances between borders since the "Louisiana Purchase," settlement of boundaries with Mexico and Canada, and the additions of Texas and California.

Previous to the days of the "Iron Horse," trading was confined to barge canal companies. The first Dow Jones Index was created in 1884, and was composed of 8 Rails and Western Union Telegraph. The Rail Index registered its orthodox top in 1906 and then formed a "flat" correction according to diagram "C" of paragraph 1, page 17 of my Treatise. Wave (A) started in 1906 at 138.36 and ended at 65.52 in 1921. Wave (B) ended at 189.11 in 1929. Wave (C) ended at 21.65 in 1940.[2] The peak of wave (B) is an "irregular" top. See graph **W** on the next page.

Graph **X** is the ratio of the Rail Index to the Industrial Index from 1906 to January 1944. This demonstrates that, in relation to the Industrials, the Rails were persistently weaker all the way from 1906 to 1940.

The causes of this behavior were:
(a) Excessive proportion of bonds to common stocks,
(b) the Panama Canal, which opened for business in 1914,
(c) the automobile and the airplane.

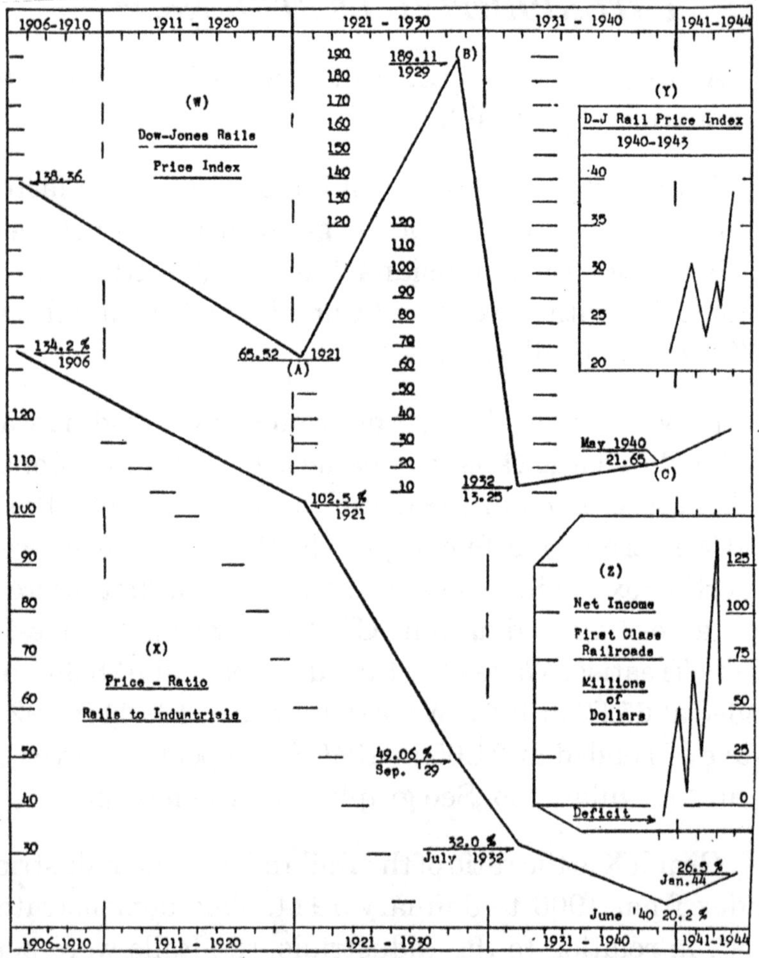

The 3 factors above mentioned resulted in weakness of both rail bonds and stocks to such an extent that in 1940 one third of rail mileage was in receivership and another third on the borderline.

The current war has temporarily removed Panama Canal competition and increased rail revenue, both passenger and freight. The extraordinary revenue that the Rails have enjoyed since 1940, especially after Pearl

Harbor, has enabled the railroad companies to reduce their bonded indebtedness and in consequence fixed charges. This benefit is permanent. See graph **X**.

The Rails registered their ratio low point in 1940 and from then to July 1943 advanced as shown in graph **Y**. The Industrials bottomed two years later, in April 1942, at the end of the 13-year triangle.

Conclusion: During the 34 year period between 1906 and 1940, the Rails reversed downward before the Industrials, and reversed upward after the Industrials. From 1940 to date this practice reversed, that is, the Rails have been first to reverse upward and last to reverse downward. This practice may continue for some years.[3]

R.N. Elliott

FOOTNOTES

[1] This letter was probably published in late January or early February of 1944.

[2] While Elliott's wave count is arguably not the best, his conclusion is correct for practical purposes. A more satisfactory wave interpretation is the one at right, presented in the January 1990 report, "Dow Jones Transportation And Utility Averages — Further Evidence Of A Developing Supercycle Degree Top in the U.S. Stock Market," by Dave Allman (available from Elliott Wave International).

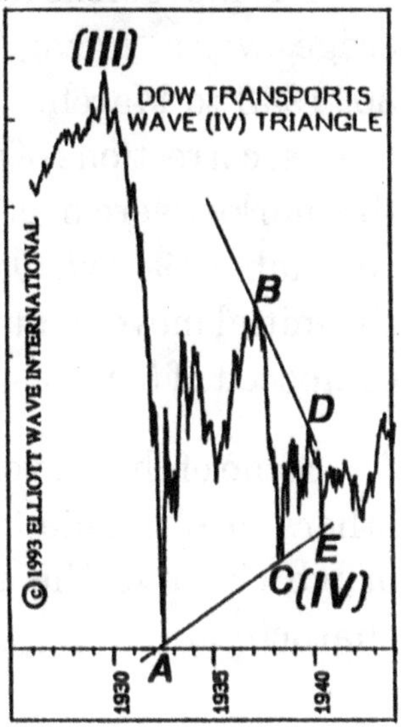

[3] This letter built upon the ideas in Interpretive Letter No. 23. See Footnote 3 thereof.

INTERPRETIVE LETTER No. 30

November 30, 1943 to March 1944

This Letter is of special importance. In the Treatise on page 17, paragraph 1, are 3 diagrams, A, B and C. They are shown below.

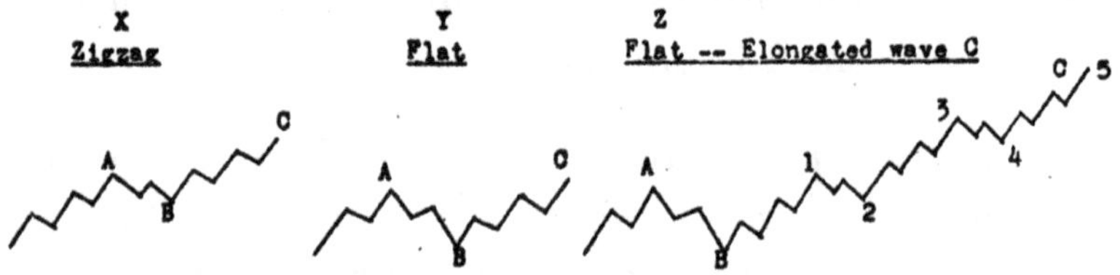

The above patterns, inverted, appear as follows:

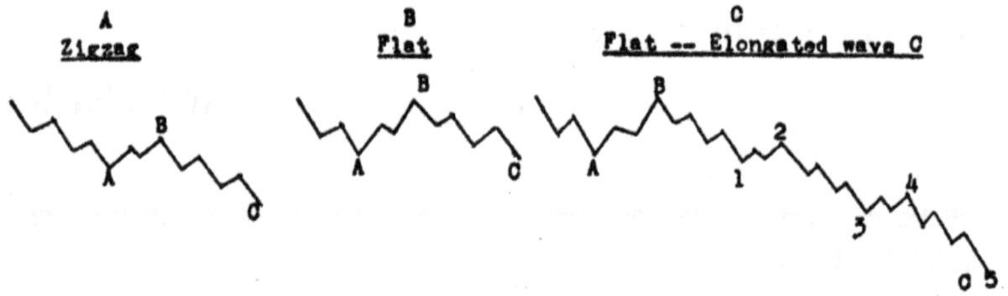

The movement from July to November 1943 in all averages was a "zigzag," as per diagram **A**. From November 30, 1943 to March, all patterns are likewise corrective, that is, corrections of corrections.[1] If from November 1943 the market were headed higher, the patterns from July to November 1943 would have been sufficient correction and the initial movement from November 30 would have been composed of 5 waves, not 3 waves as in the present case.

Some of the movements are composed of just 3 waves, others are "double 3s" and occasionally "triple 3s," all of which have the same significance, i.e., corrective character.

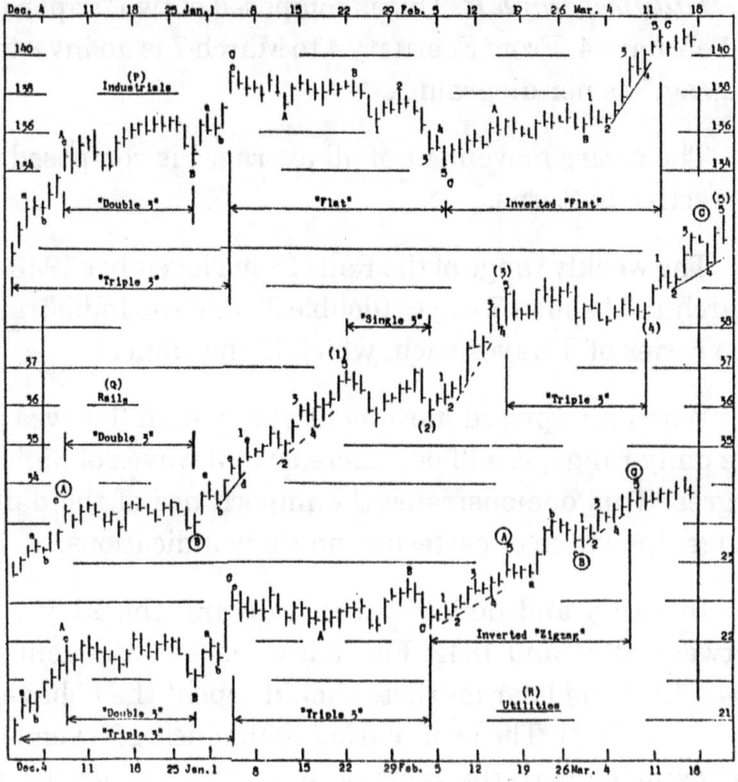

At the extreme top and bottom of the graph will be found dates of week endings. At the right side the scales are shown. The Industrials are graphed ¼" per point, Rails ½" per point, Utilities 1" per point.[2]

Industrials, graph **P**. The first movement, up to January 5th, is a "triple 3." The second movement, down to February 7, is a "flat." The third movement, up, is an inverted "flat." See diagram **Y** in paragraph 2.

Rails, graph **Q**. The first movement up to January 22nd is an inverted flat as per diagram **Y** (see paragraph 2). It might have ended there. The entire movement from November 30 to March 22 is an inverted "flat" (diagram **Z**).

Utilities, graph ***R***. This is composed of two "triple 3s" to February 4. From February 4 to March 7 is an inverted "zigzag," as per diagram **X**.

The entire movement of all averages is composed of corrective patterns.

The weekly range of the Rails from November 1943 to March 1944 shows 7 waves (double 3), and the Industrials two series of 3 waves each, which is the same.

When an upward movement starts with 3 waves in the daily range, it will end there or in 3 waves of higher degree. This demonstrates the importance of the daily range, the value of patterns and their indications.

Inflation and deflation ruled during the 21 years between 1921 and 1942. For many years subsequent to 1942, bull and bear markets should repeat the behavior preceding 1921. The bear market commencing November 1919 started with the same pattern that has developed between July 1943 and March 1944.

R.N. Elliott

FOOTNOTES

[1] Interpretive Letters Nos. 30 and 31 persist in interpreting the market as corrective, whereas in Interpretive Letter 32, he switches to the correct conclusion that a bull market advance remains in progress. Clearly the rise into approximately December 11 is a five-wave advance. Following that, Elliott is correct that the pattern is corrective, but it ends shortly after February 5.

[2] Not applicable for this book.

INTERPRETIVE LETTER No. 31

July 15, 1943 to July 10, 1944

Interpretive Letter No. 28 graphed the movement of the Dow Jones Industrial Average from April 1942 to the top of July 15, 1943, 92.69 to 146.41.

Graph U describes the weekly range of the Dow Jones Industrial Average from July 15, 1943 to July 10, 1944, 146.41 to 150.88.

On page 17 of the Treatise, following paragraph 1, are diagramed two corrective patterns, "zigzag" and "flat." For convenient reference, these are reproduced on the opposite page as diagrams **V** and **X**. An inverted "flat" is diagramed under the letter **W**.

These patterns are "corrective" and, regardless of their direction, up or down, are composed of 3 waves, a, b and c, or A, B and C. The small letters indicate waves of a lower degree than those lettered A, B and C.

The advance from April 1942 to July 1943 should be corrected by 3 waves of the same degree, i.e., waves A, B and C as in diagram **X**.

In graph **U**, waves A and B are complete, A from July to November 30, 1943 and B from November 30, 1943 to July 10, 1944. Wave C will follow. The complete pattern of waves A, B and C will be as per diagram **X**.

In graph **U**, wave A is a "zigzag" as per diagram **V**. Wave B is a "flat," inverted, as per diagram **W**. Wave C will be composed of 5 major waves downward as per wave C of diagram **X**. Minor waves 2 and 4 of C will be rallies of Minor degree. One of these rallies will be "complex" and of some importance.

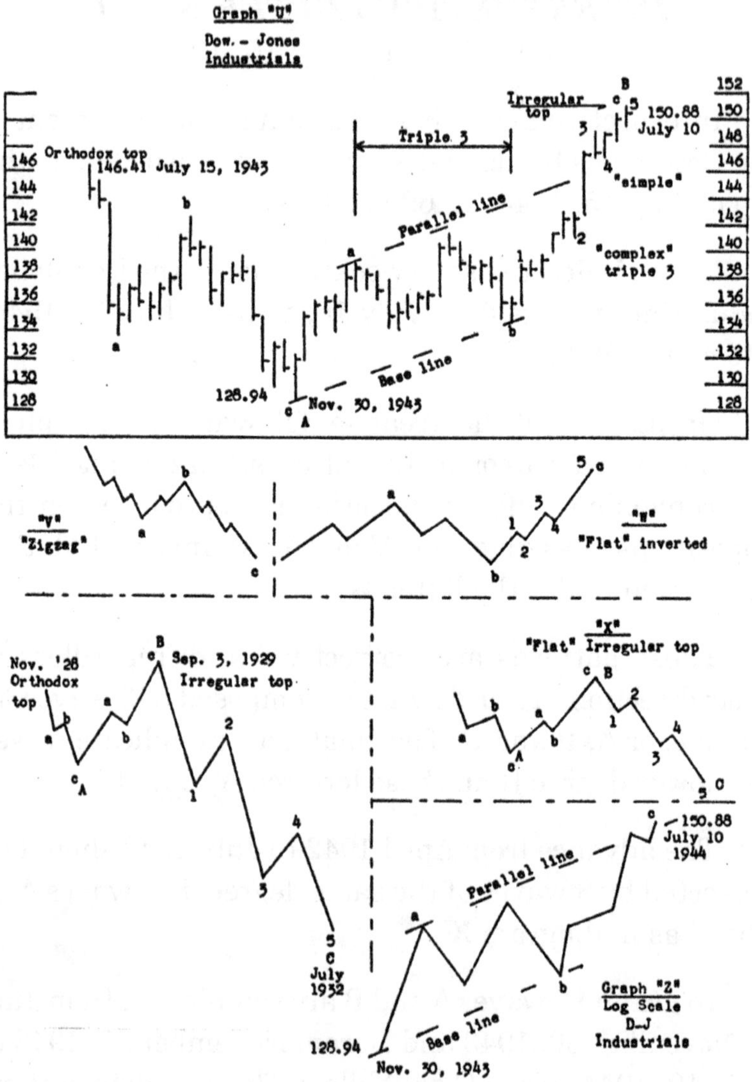

As will be noted in graph **U** and diagram **X**, wave B is higher than the beginning of wave A, that is, "irregular." As explained in the bulletin entitled "Alternation,"[1] the 1937 top was "regular"; therefore it follows that the 1944 top should be "irregular."

Interpretive Letter No. 30 demonstrated that, regardless of the extent of the movement above November 30, 1943, it would be only a rally, not the beginning of a new bull market.

For reasons demonstrated in Interpretive Letter No. 29, the Rails may decline less than the Industrials and probably reverse upward before the Industrials.

The Utilities may follow the Industrials downward, percentagewise.

Graph **Y** is an outline of the graph on page 41 of the Treatise as well as an outline of the Industrial Average from the orthodox top of November 1928 to July 1932. Wave B thereof and wave B in graph **U** are identical in pattern detail. The "irregular" top and patterns of waves A and B are also identical with those of graph **U**.

Graph **Z** is an outline on log scale of the Industrial Average from November 1943 to July 10, 1944. This is shown to demonstrate the utility of the log scale when a "throw-over" develops in the arithmetic scale, such as occurred in graph U. In graph U, wave c of B exceeded the parallel line. This is a "throw-over," as described on page 14 of the Treatise. Note that in graph **Z** there is no "throw-over" in wave c. This facilitates an accurate estimate of the top. For a complete discussion of this subject, your attention is invited to bulletin "W"[2] entitled "Gold."

R.N. Elliott

FOOTNOTES

[1] I.e., Educational Bulletin ZA, published June 7, 1944.

[2] I.e., Educational Bulletin W.

INTERPRETIVE LETTER No. 33[1]

April 28, 1942 to March 1, 1945

1.[2] The graph attached is the monthly range on arithmetic scale of the Dow Jones Industrial Average from April 28, 1942 to March 1, 1945. It is of unusual importance due to its novel pattern and because it is the first movement following the only 13 year triangle in our history.

2. The pattern is novel because the 5 Intermediate waves did not register within a channel formed by "base" and "parallel" lines.[3] Note that the 5th wave from November 1943 to March 1, 1945 followed precedent, that is, 5 waves within the channel.

3. The 3rd Intermediate wave from September 1942 to July 1943 "extended," therefore an extension is not contemplated in wave 5.

4. As demonstrated in previous releases, the numbers and ratio of the Fibonacci Summation Series apply to Time as well as to Waves and Amplitude.

5. Horizontal arrows below the graph show the number of months duration from different points to February 1945. All the Time Periods, 5, 8, 13, 21[4] and 34 months respectively, are Fibonacci numbers. When two or more Time Periods terminate simultaneously, reversal is indicated. The greater the number of Time Periods terminating simultaneously, and the larger the Time Units (days, weeks, months or years), the more important the reversal.

6. Time Periods are not exact for the reason that months vary in length, and all the Fibonacci numbers

(except 5) carry fractions.[5] Moreover, movements seldom commence or end with the calendar month. Therefore, a slight tolerance is admissible. For obvious reasons, weekly Time Periods are more exact.

7. The ruling ratio of the Fibonacci numbers is 61.8%. The amplitude of wave ⑤ is 61.8% of the amplitude of waves ① and ③.[6]

8. All of these features are demonstrated in my bulletin entitled "Nature's Law."[7]

R.N. Elliott

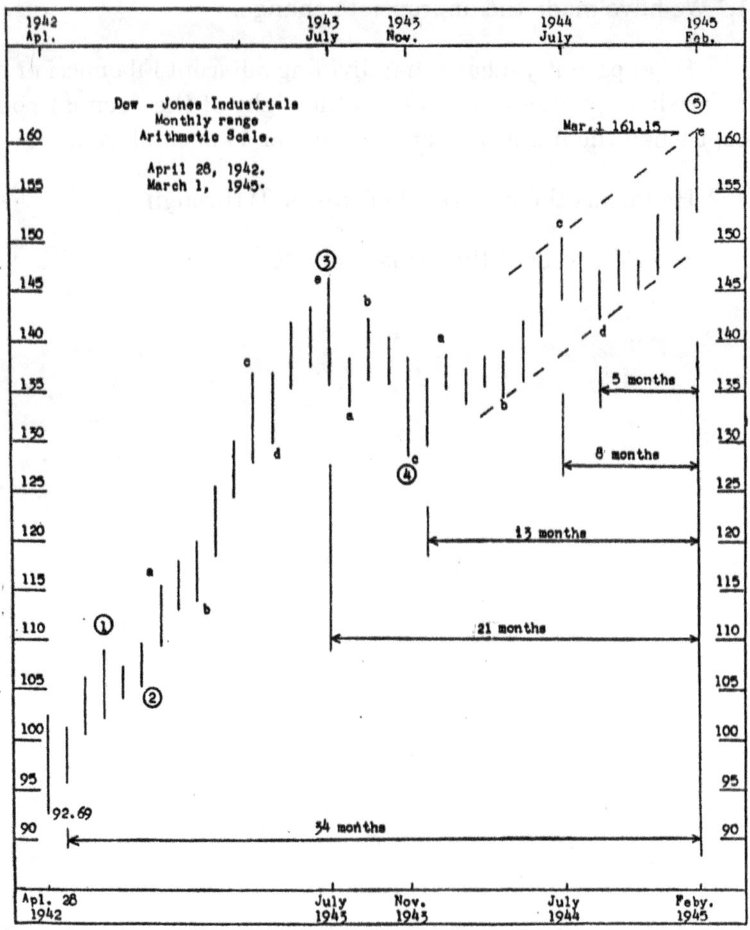

FOOTNOTES

[1] Interpretive Letter No. 32 is not available.

[2] Elliott returned to numbering his paragraphs at this time. They often totaled 8.

[3] Rather than quickly concluding that the pattern is novel, Elliott would have done better to label the peak in July 1943 as a first wave, the 1943 low as a second wave, with a developing third in progress. A channel is ultimately better served this way. The supposed novelty was a message that the wave wasn't over.

[4] Elliott's original chart had the label "34" where he wanted "21." We have made the appropriate change.

[5] He apparently means that dividing adjacent Fibonacci numbers produces endless numbers to the right of the decimal point except when the number 5 (or the number 1) is employed.

[6] He means the net travel of waves ① through ③.

[7] See Educational Bulletins X and Z.

CONFIDENTIAL
March 7, 1945

Dow-Jones Averages

Industrials	*Rails*	*Utilities*
Tops, 162.22 Mar 6	52.87 Mar 6	27.67 Mar 2

Based on the Time Factor, my Confidential Letter of January 31, 1945[1] forecast top for the Industrials during February 1945. This is now confirmed by waves, but in a novel pattern demonstrated by the graph in Interpretive Letter No. 33, enclosed.

Extensive buying of low priced stocks occurred.[2] Numerous "split-ups" suggest distribution. New York stock exchanges have raised margin requirements on low priced stocks. Mr. Eccles, Chairman of the Federal Reserve Board, recently expressed his opinion that inflation threatens and that something should be done to prevent it. Mr. Morganthau, Secretary of the Treasury, agrees with Mr. Eccles. Thus far, waves of the Industrial Average do not confirm their views. However, if the corrective bear market is sub-normal (very short), then inflation will be a fact.[3]

The two sub-normal bear markets of the Industrials during the 'Twenties were composed of 20 and 25 points respectively. A normal bear market would be about 40 points. See my bulletin entitled "Nature's Law,"[4] especially the final paragraph.

Reversal is now due, but on account of the novel pattern from April 1942, to date, I hesitate making a prediction as to how serious the correction may be.

The Utilities follow the Industrials. The Rails led the recent advance, as forecast they would in the "Conclusion" of Interpretive Letter No. 29.

In conclusion, I recommend that all common stocks be sold immediately.[5] Even if the reversal is sub-normal, reentry should be possible below present prices.

R.N. Elliott

PD: On the chart in Interpretive Letter No. 33, the extreme top should read "March 6, 162.22" instead of "March 1, 161.15."

FOOTNOTES

[1] Not available.

[2] This behavior is more often a characteristic of first, third and "B" waves than of fifth waves.

[3] Elliott here extends his original concept of "inflation," as first presented in Educational Bulletin U (see Footnote 1 with that letter), to say that it reflects the presence of monetary inflation. As discussed in *Elliott Wave Principle*, however, speed, persistence and extent of advance in the stock market is not an indication of the presence of monetary inflation. In fact, if anything, an inverse relationship is suggested by the data.

[4] See Educational Bulletins X and Z.

[5] A minor top is indeed being registered and a sharp sell off ensues. However, Elliott's attempts to call a major top are premature.

INTERPRETIVE LETTER No. 34[1]
Psychology
August 6, 1945

Natural resources, climate, genius and democracy of the United States required the formation of corporations to finance individual initiative. Stock exchanges are the natural medium to accomplish the flotation of corporations.

The New York Stock Exchange is by far the largest, on which are listed some 1300 issues. Its marvelous machinery and organization reflect psychology immediately and to perfection.

On the next page[2] are shown two graphs covering the period from April 1942 (the end of the 13-year triangle) to July 1945.

The lower graph is my "Psychology" index of all stocks listed on the Exchange.[3] The pattern is perfect and as diagramed in my Treatise on page 17, paragraph 3, extreme right. Note the 5 Major waves (1, 2, 3, 4 and 5 encircled). The 5th wave "extended," as indicated by the numbers 1, 2, 3, 4 and 5 (not encircled). The "extended" 5th wave extended as shown by small letters a, b, c, d and e.[4] The entire movement completely filled the channel formed by "Base" and "Parallel" Lines. The 5th Major wave is the same length as waves 1 and 3 combined.

The upper graph is the Dow Jones Industrial Average. The 5th wave ended at 169.55 and was only 75% of the first 3 waves. If it had touched the Parallel Line, it would have reached 185, or 15 points higher. I can only surmise why it failed.

The New York Stock Exchange publishes the market value of all stocks listed as of the end of each month. These figures show that the value for June 1945 equalled that of March 1937, which proves that the "Psychology" index is correct.

R.N. Elliott

FOOTNOTES

[1] It is not known for certain whether further Interpretive Letters were issued, but the lack of further issues is consistent with the fact that Elliott began assembling "Nature's Law" at this time. It was published ten months later.

[2] Not available

[3] This is an update of the chart shown in Educational Bulletin P, some detail of which was shown in Interpretive Letter No. 24 as graph Y.

[4] Again, Elliott would have avoided misinterpretation with one fundamental change toward expecting extended third rather than extended fifth waves. The actual high is due several months hence. This error leads Elliott to find several "irregular tops" when actually a fifth wave, usually smaller than a third, is terminating.

CONFIDENTIAL

July 23, 1946[1]

Dow-Jones Averages

	High Point	*Close July 19*
Industrials:	213.36 May 29	201.13
Rails:	68.77 June 17	62.98
Utilities	43.95 May 29	40.72

Hereafter, when references to the "Treatise" are cited, please refer to the new edition entitled, "Nature's Law."

Please review the "Notes" at bottom of page 60, and diagrams of an "irregular" top on page 23.

The market is now in wave "C" of[2] the "irregular" top.

You will be promptly advised when and what to purchase for the next advance.

R.N. Elliott

FOOTNOTES

[1] Elliott has just, in June, published his second monograph. From this date forward only one publication survives, the last Educational Bulletin published herein, entitled "Miracle of the Ages", which was published on December 20, 1946. Its content suggests that indeed nothing was published in between.

[2] He means, "following" the irregular top which was wave "B". Regardless, Elliott's outlook is correct, and his clients avoided the crash of August-September to below his "A" wave low of February.

Educational Bulletins and Circulars

THE WAVE PRINCIPLE

63 WALL STREET
NEW YORK

R. N. ELLIOTT

The **WAVE PRINCIPLE** is a Law of Nature, - not a theory or gadget.

Actions and Reactions of Major, Intermediate and Minor movements are catalogued.

Investors and traders are given the position of the market.

Two Services are available, - Forecast and Educational.

The **FORECAST** Service is in the form of definite recommendations issued when developments indicate. These Letters are brief, positive and devoid of tedious discussion of events, statistics, etc.

It serves two purposes:

(a) For those who are too busy with their own affairs to study The Wave Principle.

(b) For students who wish to take advantage of my current recommendations regarding market movements but have not yet acquired sufficient proficiency to act on their own initiative.

The **EDUCATIONAL** Service consists of surveys in which market movements are charted and their waves classified in accordance with my Treatise and are therefore valuable for all time. New subscribers are furnished with reference file and bulletins on general subjects such as Trading Media, Charting, Timing, etc. This service is unique and economical for the reason that the subscriber may become independent of services for all time. SEE REVERSE SIDE FOR FURTHER EXPLANATION.

The Treatise is a text book and discloses the behavior of market cycles as they have been and will be for all time.

The regular fees are:		
	Treatise	$ 3.00*
	Educational Service	57.50 annually*
	Forecast Service	97.50 annually*
	Combined services	152.50 annually*

**(These services currently available if you prefer them to the offer below)*

To new subscribers I offer a copy of my Treatise and both Services up to May 1st, 1945 for $37.50. Regardless of the date accepted, the expiration of subscriptions at this special rate will be May 1st, 1945.

November 6, 1944

R. N. Elliott.

- -

Date........................194

To - R. N. Elliott,
63 Wall Street, New York (5), N. Y.

I accept your special offer of November 6th, 1944 and enclose $37.50 for which send me your Treatise and both sèrvices to May 1st, 1945.

Address

Name ....

....

MARKET MOVEMENTS REPEAT IN IDENTICAL WAVES

These waves are uniform because they reflect a natural law; a law known as far back as early Greece; a law that operates, not only in the stock market, but throughout the animate and inanimate world.

Thus, the broad pattern of one bull market conforms to the pattern of another; the broad pattern of one bear market, to the pattern of all other bear markets. Compare, for instance, the bull swing of the 'Twenties with the bull swing of the 'Thirties and observe the identical wave formation.

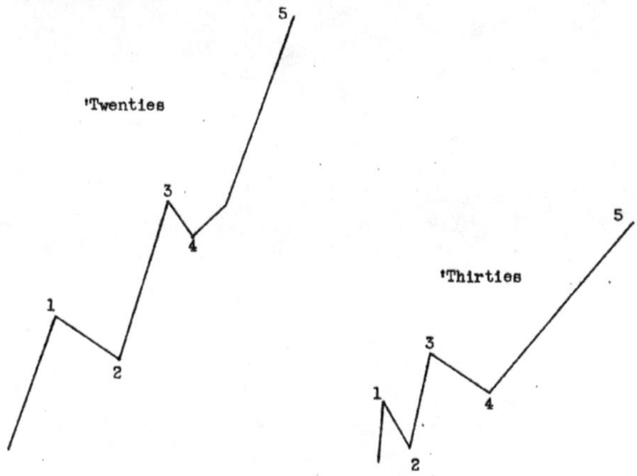

My Educational service completely acquaints the student of stock market phenomena with the laws of the wave movement, of which the above is a simple illustration. It is designed to so thoroughly train him in reading current trends and forecasting pending trends - minor, intermediate, and major in character. Thus, those who learn the valuable principles of this fundamental law need no longer rely on others for market advice but can read and project the market for themselves.

During the period that the wave movement is being taught, my forecasting service, working entirely with the law of the wave movement, accompanies the educational service. Thus, it offers market guidance during that period when the subscriber is in process of learning wave movement phenomena, and it is likewise interpretative in character, thus further grounding the subscriber in the important principles under discussion. This forecasting service points out market trends and, at important turning points, gives specific stocks for purchase or sale.

BECAUSE THE WAVE PRINCIPLE SHOWS THE STOCK MARKET AS NOW BEING AT A MOST IMPORTANT POINT, THE FORECASTING SERVICE, I BELIEVE, SHOULD PROVE OF GREAT BENEFIT TO STOCK MARKET OPERATORS. ACCORDINGLY, I SUGGEST THAT YOU TAKE IMMEDIATE ADVANTAGE OF THE OFFER ON THE REVERSE SIDE.

Selection of Trading Mediums

December 15, 1939

My circular of November 20, 1939[1] demonstrated that the factor of first importance in stock trading is *timing*, that is, *when* to buy and sell. The factor of next importance was mentioned, i.e., in *what* stocks to trade. This current circular elaborates on the latter subject.

To guide you in selecting securities (either stocks or bonds) in which trading is contemplated, you should keep uppermost in mind all of the following fundamentals.

1. Fluctuations and Income: Fluctuations in market value of any security are much greater than their income yield. Therefore, the paramount factor is the preservation and appreciation of principal as a result of price fluctuations.

2. Bull Market Tops: In bull markets, each group of the 55 Standard Statistics list shows tops made at different times, like a fan. Bull markets are those which develop five primary waves during a period of about five years. During such a period, the several groups tend to move rather uniformly, being propelled by the powerful force of the cycle.

3. Bear Markets: Usually the duration of a bear market is longer than the previous bull market.[2] During the severe and relatively short duration of the decline from 1929 to 1932, the very best stocks and bonds, as well as the lower grades of both, had to be liquidated regardless of their real value. Many traders gained the erroneous impression that the bottoms of *all* bear markets should repeat that performance. Research indicates many years will elapse before such a drastic decline may be expected. The final bottoms of bear markets are conspicuous by bottoms of nearly all groups being made at one time. This is just the reverse of tops in bull markets. During bear markets, powerful leadership is less pronounced, and this is especially true during rallies. During bear market cycles, the market as a whole and the several groups become more sensitive to current events and extraneous factors. Between January 26 and July 28, 1939, the London Industrial average formed a triangle. The downward thrust immediately following caused a suspension of the advancing cycle that was under way on the New York Stock Exchange. This notable example was forecast and explained in my Letters.[3] A somewhat similar phenomenon, but due to other causes, occurred in 1922 and 1933.

4. *Previous Experience in Trading*: Many traders acquire prejudices against certain stocks because of previous unfortunate experiences. To pursue such a course, the trader would eventually find no group free from objection.

5. *Inactive Stocks*: A stock that is frequently or occasionally inactive should be avoided for trading, the reason being that public psychology does not have an opportunity to register the Wave impulse. Inactivity clearly indicates that the stock does not enjoy thorough distribution or else that it has reached the fully developed stage described in paragraph 7 (c).

6. *Inside Tips*: Almost always, inside tips from well intentioned friends refer to inactive and low priced stocks, but it should be borne in mind that mass psychology is essential to influence the market price. It is therefore preferable to confine one's trading to stocks that are always active.

7. *The Age of Stocks*: The life of a stock usually has three stages:

(a) The first is the youthful or experimental stage, during which such stocks should be avoided, as they have not been properly seasoned.

(b) The second is the creative stage, and stocks that fall within this category have reached healthy development, thus making them a desirable medium for trading, provided they are thoroughly seasoned.

(c) The third or grown-up stage represents the period of fullest development. Dividends may be uniformly reliable and fluctuations narrow. For these reasons, the certificates become lodged in portfolios and therefore the stock becomes less attractive for trading purposes.

Summary of Above Recommendations

When the pattern of a reliable average is favorable under The Wave Principle, follow the recommendations below:

A. Select the groups which perform in harmony with the average.

B. Then select stocks that move in sympathy with these groups.

C. Always choose stocks that are constantly active, medium priced and seasoned leaders.

D. Diversify your funds. I.e., employ more or less an equal number of dollars in from five to ten stocks, not more than one stock of a group, for example:

General Motors	U. S. Steel
United Aircraft	New York Central
U.S. Rubber	Con. Edison.

Trading in less than five stocks is preferable to more than ten stocks.

R.N. Elliott

FOOTNOTES

[1] A copy of the actual page published is unavailable, but it is unlikely that there were any significant differences between it and the section entitled "Investment Timing" (listed as "Timing of Investment" on the Contents page) published in "Nature's Law" and reprinted in *R.N. Elliott's Masterworks*.

[2] See Footnote 6 in Interpretive Letter No. 8, which was written just prior to this one.

[3] See Interpretive Letter No. 9.

Charting

December 20, 1939

The subject of charting price fluctuations is discussed on pages 24 and 26 of the Treatise entitled “The Wave Principle,” but students might benefit by more detailed suggestions which I have found essential in the extensive plotting that has been done. Several model charts are shown on the next page.

Lines to Portray the Daily Price Range

To accurately observe the lower degrees of waves of a movement, The Wave Principle requires the Daily Range of the high-low price fluctuations. This high-low range was inaugurated by Dow Jones in 1928.

The chart spacings mentioned below are recommended for the purpose of emphasizing price fluctuations:

a vertical quarter inch for one point of the Industrial Average,
a vertical half inch for one point of the Rail Average,
a vertical half inch for one point of the Utility Average.

Such spacings on a chart facilitate accurate interpretation, whereas a short vertical range may create uncertainty.

The quarter inch scale is subdivided into fifths, thus eliminating any guess work as to the exact spot at which to locate the Daily Range and Hourly Record.

Likewise, it is important to space the distance between days as shown on the model charts. When each vertical line of the chart is employed instead of every other line, the result is that lines of the price range are too cramped for comfortable reading. Do not leave any space for casual holidays.

The Hourly Record

Precisely the same quarter inch scale and forms are recommended for the Hourly Record, one quarter of an inch horizontally for a session of five hours, or one of the smallest squares for each hour. Do not leave any space following a two hour session on Saturday. Do not show the opening figure. The high-low range for the day should be shown at the end of the last hour of each session.

All of these recommendations are portrayed on the charts on the next page.

Chart Paper

Never economize in chart paper at the expense of clarity. When a movement begins on one sheet and terminates on another, clarity is jeopardized. The same is true when a movement is discontinued at the top of the sheet and started again at the bottom.

Chart paper which will properly clarify interpretation of waves is manufactured by Keuffel & Esser[1] and is for sale by them and by large stationery stores. It is available in these sizes:

by the yard, 20" wide,
in sheets 8 1/2" x 11",
in sheets 10" x 15".

Two weights of paper in all three sizes are offered.

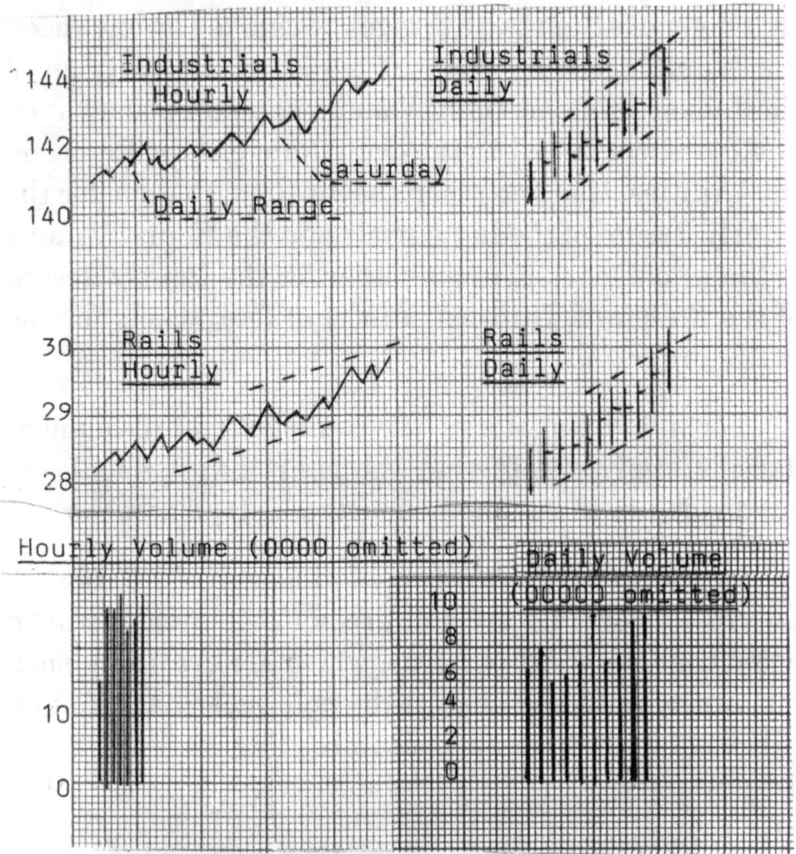

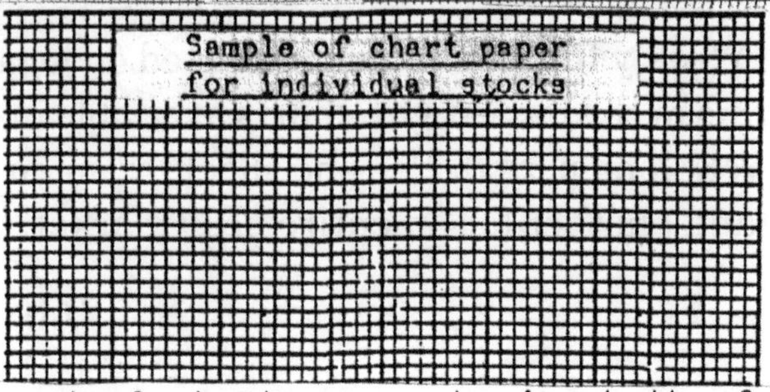

On the actual chart paper showing both of these for the cross coded times are pale green in color and it will be noted that the chart patterns which are drawn in black ink are accentuated against the pale green background which is highly advantageous in reading waves.

It is suggested that charts 10" x 15" be used, and that not more than two averages be charted on one sheet. For example, on one sheet 10" x 15", the Daily Range of the Industrials and Daily Volume should be shown; on another sheet 10" x 15", the Daily Range of the Rails and the Utilities. Use two other sheets 10" x 15", one for the Hourly Record of the Industrials and the Hourly Volume of the whole market, and another for the Hourly Record of the Rails and Utilities, a total of four sheets for the entire program.

For individual stocks, the same general recommendations apply except that the chart paper should be subdivided in the ruling by fourths instead of fifths.

On the actual chart paper showing both of these forms, the cross ruled lines are pale green in color and it will be noted that the chart patterns, which are drawn in black ink, are accentuated against the pale green background, which is highly advantageous in reading waves.

Weekly Range

The Weekly Range should be charted on logarithmic scale forms in the largest size charts available in order to cover a very long period. Use one sheet for an entire bull market and another for an entire bear market.

R.N. Elliott

FOOTNOTES

[1] Still available.

EDUCATIONAL BULLETIN A[1]

The underlying forces that produce price trends are dominated and controlled by a Natural Law. This fundamental law cannot be subverted or set aside by statutes or restrictions. Current news and political developments are of only incidental importance, soon forgotten; their presumed influence on market trends is not as weighty as is commonly believed.

After years of intensive studies of cyclical price movements, their causes and behavior, the writer observed a rhythmic regularity in all series of price changes. These rhythmic changes were classified. Finally there evolved certain principles, which were carefully tested back over a long period of years. The highly important discoveries made are fully discussed in the copyrighted treatise, "The Wave Principle."

The Wave Principle has now been used successfully for several years in the management of investment funds,[2] and in forecasting the important major and intermediate trends. A series of articles, revealing the broad workings of The Wave Principle, was published in *The Financial World* during June, July and August 1939.[3]

The Wave Principle is not a "market" system or theory. The application of the Principle in market analysis is shown in the accompanying chart[4] of the weekly price ranges (Dow Jones Industrial Average) for the 1932-1937 bull market. The various important "turning points," including the final top, were clearly indicated, together with their significance as to degree, by this phenomenon. During this entire five-year period, The Wave Principle measured and forecast these various phases without deviation from the law of precedents as revealed in the Treatise.

The Educational Service is available for serious investors, who intend, with preliminary guidance in the application of The Wave Principle to the various phases and trends of the market as they occur, to acquire complete mastery of the subject. Such mastery will enable subscribers to the Educational Service to use The Wave Principle for guiding their own investment programs independently.

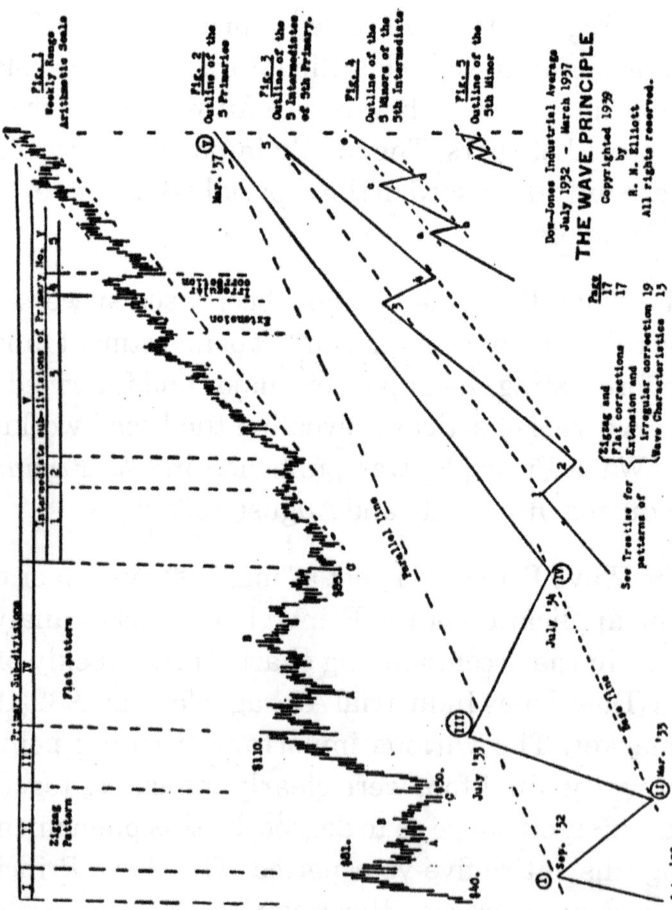

The Investment Forecasting Service is available for investors whose time is so occupied that they are dependent upon expert advice for profitable management of their investments. In this service clients are advised when to buy and sell.

R.N. Elliott

FOOTNOTES

1 The publication date appears to be late December 1939 or early January 1940.

2 This is the only reference to fund management in Elliott's writings. Independent sources confirm that he managed some accounts.

3 Reprinted in *R.N. Elliott's Masterworks*.

4 On the chart, you will notice that Intermediate waves 2 and 4 of Primary wave Ⓥ do not alternate. Since wave C of Ⓘⓥ does not fall below A, it is acceptable, if not preferable, to label the next eight weeks as waves D and E of a triangle. If that is done, then the end of Intermediate wave 1 is better labeled at the peak price shown as part of Elliott's Intermediate wave 2. Alternation is then satisfied within Primary wave Ⓥ.

EDUCATIONAL BULLETIN B[1]
Cycles

Numerous explanations have been offered by economists and market analysts to account for the peculiar behavior of the stock market from July 25, 1939, in its downward movement, to the outbreak of the war on September 1, at which time a buying stampede set in, and its subsequent reactions to January 15, 1940.[2] The simplest and only reliable answer, and the one that means the difference between profits and losses, is contained in the word "cycle."

There is usually a certain parallel connection between the trends of business and stock prices. However, correct forecasts of coming changes in either of them are possible only by careful analysis of the action of the cycle of each one individually, irrespective of external conditions.[3]

The term "cycle," as defined in "The Wave Principle," refers to the distance between start and finish of a completed trend or movement.[4] The large chart on the next page shows clearly how a "cycle" pattern is formed. The rhythm determines when the cycle is completed. A cyclical movement includes certain component parts. These are known as Primary, Intermediate and Minor waves. Numbers and letters are placed at wave endings.

Bull markets are composed of five Primary waves. Each of the advancing Primary waves (odd numbers 1, 3 and 5) is composed of five Intermediate waves. Each advancing Intermediate wave is composed of five Minor waves.

Bear markets are composed of three Primary waves, but are variable in detailed composition. The bear market shown on the opposite page is called a "zigzag" pattern.

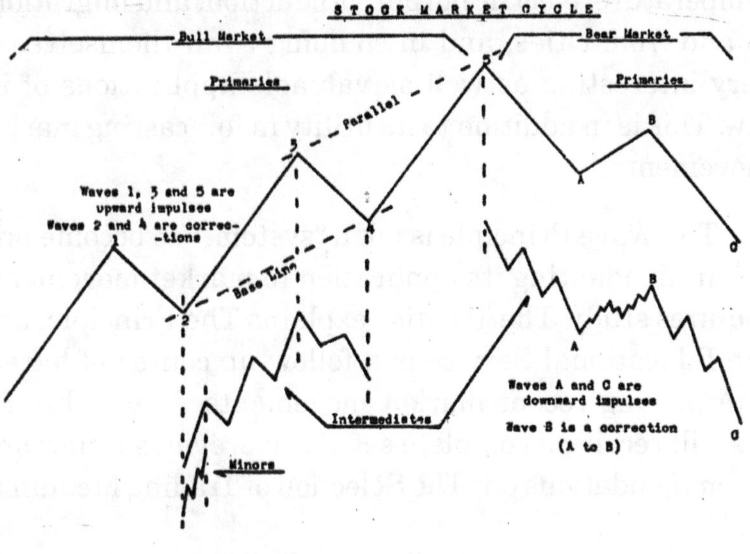

Numbers and Letters are placed at wave endings.

Correction in bull markets (even numbers 2 and 4) have the same characteristics in lesser degrees.

This rhythmic regularity is the key to the natural law that dominates and controls market movements.

The Wave Principle is a phenomenon that was discovered only after years of intensive study of market behavior. The Principle has been carefully tested and used successfully by subscribers in forecasting market movements.

If so inclined, students may readily apply The Wave Principle to many other broad subjects such as

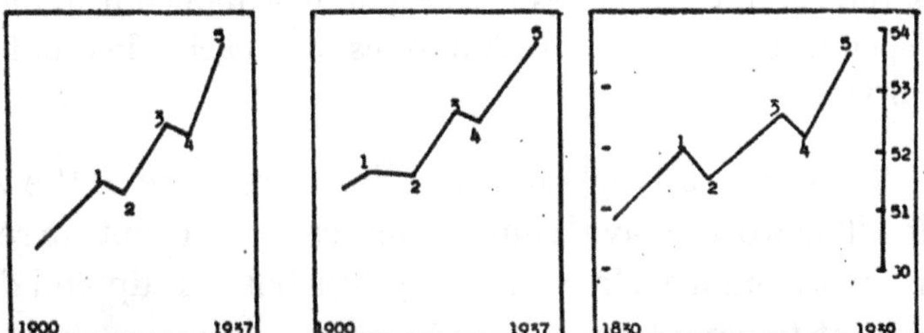

Copper World Production — Cotton World Production — National Industrial Conference Board

Temperature Mean Average by Decades in New York City

temperature, electric output, production, and migrations to and from cities, and in so doing avail themselves of very interesting as well as valuable applications of its law. This is in addition to its utility in forecasting market movements.

The Wave Principle is not a "system." To become proficient in adapting its application to market movements requires study. The Treatise explains The Principle, and the Educational Service is a follow-up course of letters interpreting recent market movements. New subscribers will receive a complete set of the previous issues and recommendations on "The Selection of Trading Mediums" and "Charting."

The Forecast Service gives specific and timely market recommendations.

R.N. Elliott

FOOTNOTES

[1] The publication date appears to be January 16, 1940.

[2] See Interpretive Letters Nos. 9 through 11.

[3] This crucially important point, which contradicts conventional wisdom even today, is reiterated in Educational Bulletins C and V. Elliott himself would have handled some of the analysis in his Interpretative Letters better had he extended it to include the dependence of various stock indexes from each other and from bond prices.

[4] There is really no point in Elliott's redefining the word "cycle." The word "wave" communicates the concept correctly, as distinct from a cycle, which requires both an up and down movement to complete.

EDUCATIONAL BULLETIN C[1]
The Law of Motion

Heretofore, attention has been mainly directed toward cyclical rhythm in the stock market, where it is very pronounced. Every movement, from wheels to planets, is necessarily cyclical. All cycles have fixed subdivisions peculiar to each, which facilitates a measurement of their progress. It now appears opportune to discuss cyclical rhythm in general.

Planets: Each planet travels in its own orbit and at a speed peculiar to itself. The Earth revolves on its own axis once every 24 hours, and this divides night from day. It encircles the sun once a year and thus affords the four seasons. The mechanism of planetariums may be turned backward or forward to show the relative positions and movements of planets and their satellites at any time, past, present and future. I recommend accepting the first opportunity to visit one.

Elements: Apparently some of these never change their form, while others do. For example, water, in its flow, constantly performs complete cycles. The sun's rays on the ocean's surface cause water to vaporize. Air currents move the vapor until it encounters cooler atmosphere over hills and mountains, which in turn condenses the vapor. Gravity draws the water back to earth where it again joins the sea.

Nations experience political, cultural and economic cycles, both great and small.

Human Life: Another cycle, "from dust to dust," is subdivided into Childhood, Productive Period and Decadence. Wave Principle patterns are observed in mass movements such as migrations to and from cities, average age, birth rate, etc.

Human Activities: These are numerous and, like planets, travel in their own orbit and at speeds peculiar to each. My circular entitled "Cycles" shows a "Stock Market Cycle," the pattern of which conforms to rules which apply to all human activities. A casual glance at the graphs below will demonstrate that one phase of activity cannot be depended upon to reliably forecast another. Therefore, the cycle of each pattern must be analyzed by itself as to position, by its own waves, and not by extraneous elements.[2] During the last quarter of 1939, the lag of the stock market curve

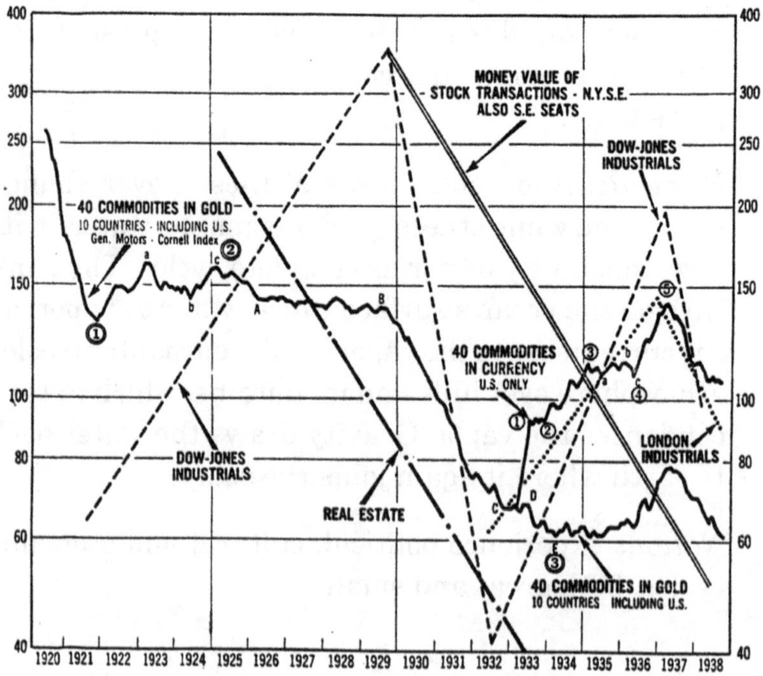

to that of business produced much discussion but no explanation. The only known method is to observe the phenomenon as disclosed in my Treatise on The Wave Principle.

The graph of "Temperature" in the circular on "Cycles" is of transcendental importance. Atmospheric temperature cannot be affected by Human Activities; nevertheless, cyclical waves over a period of 110 years formed a perfect Wave Principle pattern.

You prepare for approaching night and the seasons of the year. Why not prepare for the future by learning the pattern behavior of cycles, instead of exhausting your energies and substance by "guessing"?

The Wave Principle cannot be learned overnight, but handsomely rewards those who study it.

R.N. Elliott

FOOTNOTES

[1] The publication date was apparently between February and June, 1940. The out-of-date chart suggests that some of this material was taken from an earlier exposition, perhaps a letter to Collins.

[2] See Footnote 2 with Educational Bulletin B.

The Basis of The Wave Principle[1]

October 1, 1940

Civilization rests upon change. This change is cyclical in origin and characteristics. A rhythmic series of extreme changes constitutes a cycle. When a cycle has been completed, another cycle is started. The rhythm of the new cycle will be the same as that of the previous cycle, although the extent and duration may vary. The cycle progresses in accordance with the natural law of movement.

This law of natural change is inevitable, and applies to the seasons and the movements of the tides and planets. It has truly been said that change is the only "immutable thing in life." Being a natural phenomenon, it necessarily governs all human activities, even the relatively static sciences of biology and botany. Even time and mathematics appear to be amenable to the application of this law of rhythm, from the small unit of hours to the great intervals of decades, centuries and millenniums.

The causes of these cyclical changes seem clearly to have their origin in the immutable natural law that governs all things, including the various moods of human behavior. Causes, therefore, tend to become relatively unimportant in the long term progress of the cycle.

Measuring the behavior of cycles should therefore offer a reliable means of forecasting changes, regardless of the cause, and thus yield handsome profits. After extensive studies of changes in the stock market over a period of many years, I discovered a clue that measures and determines cyclical trends.

By 1934, I was able to resolve the various trends of changes in stock prices to a rhythmic series of component waves, which I called a "cycle." This cyclical rhythm has occurred regularly and repeatedly not only in the available records of the various stock exchanges, but also in commodities, industrial production, temperature, music, variation in color, electric output, population movements to and from cities, etc. In fact, it is manifest so widely, not only in human activities, but also in the workings of nature itself, that I have termed this discovery "The Wave Principle."

The number of waves and the extent and duration of movements seem clearly to be allied with the principle of mathematics and with the passage of time, but the number of waves never varies except under certain recognizable conditions of a cyclical nature. The *length* of a wave may possibly be affected by emotional news, but the *number* of waves is clearly not affected by such transient developments. By means of this rhythmic analysis, the end of a movement is known as it approaches, and the type of the next movement is also known. It is therefore possible to predict with confidence when a bull market is terminating and a bear market is beginning, or vice versa.

On the following page are shown three graphs of a stock market cycle, including the constructive phases of a bull market, and the destructive phases of a bear market. The number of waves in a cycle is also compared with the mathematical principles laid down centuries ago by Pythagoras and Fibonacci.

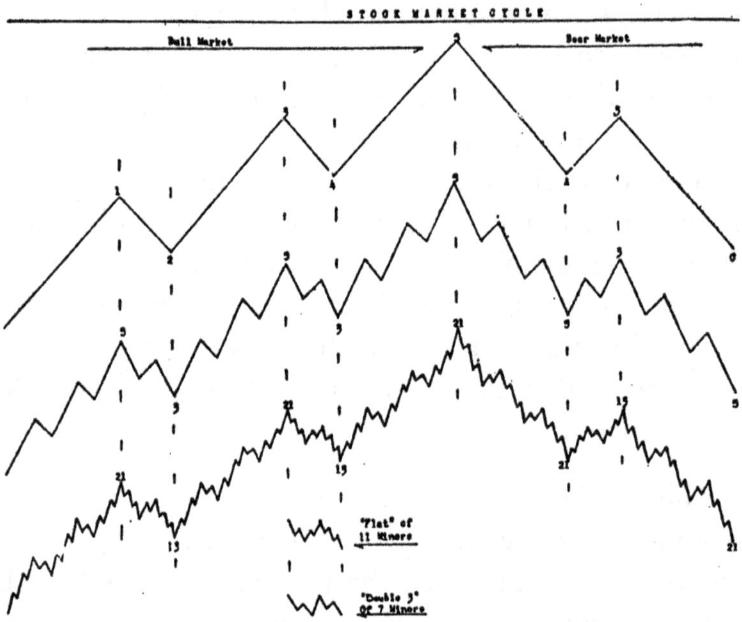

How The Wave Principle Works, and its Correlation with Mathematical Laws

The graph at the top outlines the fundamental or largest waves of a complete cycle. There are five waves in the bull market, and three waves in the bear market.

In the middle graph, these same eight fundamental waves are amplified to show their component waves, totaling 34. Note the constancy of the "five-three" rhythm. This graph shows the Intermediate stages of a cycle.

The third graph is simply a more detailed analysis of the same 8 fundamental, or 34 intermediate, waves of a cycle, including the 89 minor waves of a bull market and the 55 minor waves of a bear market. The total is 144. Again the "five-three" relationship holds true. A corrective phase of the cycle will occasionally vary the rhythm slightly for the minor waves, and in such instances, the count will be 7 or 11, according to the type or pattern, which indicates what is happening.

The basis of The Wave Principle is very old. Pythagoras in the sixth century B.C., Fibonacci in the thirteenth century and many other scientists, including Leonardo da Vinci and Marconi, have all shown that they were aware to some extent of this phenomenon. Fibonacci was an Italian mathematician, also known as Leonardo da Pisa. His "Summation Series of Dynamic Symmetry" agrees in every respect with the rhythmic count of the Wave Principle, and the number of waves is the same.

Fibonacci apparently derived his Summation Series from the famous Pythagorean diagram of a pyramid, consisting of ten units, beginning with one and ending with four. This diagram, Pythagoras said, was the "Key to the Secret of the Universe." Not only can this diagram be applied to the seasons of the year, but also to the great inner cycles of the well known ten-year cycle.[2]

The similarity of The Wave Principle, the Fibonacci Summation Series and the Pythagorean diagram is shown in the tables on the next page.

It should be noted that when I discovered The Wave Principle action of market trends, I had never heard of either the Fibonacci Series or of the Pythagorean Diagram.[3] It is naturally gratifying to me that these old mathematical principles that were laid down centuries ago simply substantiate the validity of a present day application of basic law to practical use.

As to the conformance of the time element, or duration of market trends, with the rhythm of The Wave Principle, many "coincidences" can be cited.

R. N. Elliott

The Wave Principle					Fibonacci Summation Series
Graphs	Degree	Number of Waves in: Bull Market	Bear Market	Total Cycle	
					1+ 2 = 3
Top	Primaries	5	3	8	
					2+ 3 = 5
		5	5		
		3	3		3+ 5 = 8
Middle	Interme-	5	5		
	diates	3			5+ 8 = 13
		5			
		21	13	34	8+13 = 21
		21	21		13+21 = 34
Bottom	Minors	13			
		21	13		21+34 = 55
		13			
		21	21		34+55 = 89
		89	55	144	
					55+89=144

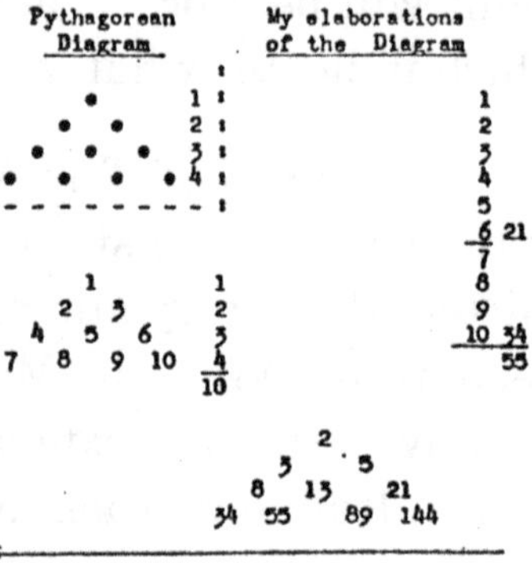

FOOTNOTES

[1] This and the next treatise are unlettered, but are included here due to their chronology.

[2] He is probably referring the the Decennial Pattern. See the discussion in *Elliott Wave Principle.*

[3] Charles J. Collins introduced Elliott to these ideas by way of some material sent in 1934, as noted in the biography in *R.N. Elliott's Masterworks*. In 1940, Elliott made the connection between them and his Wave Principle.

[1]Market Apathy — Cause and Termination[2]

August 11, 1941

The total yearly volume of stock transactions on the New York Stock Exchange has been declining for five consecutive years, and apathy has been most pronounced since October 1939. The causes of this apathy can be traced to cyclical influences and measured mathematically. Sustained market activity expands or contracts with the length of the price trend. The longer the trend,

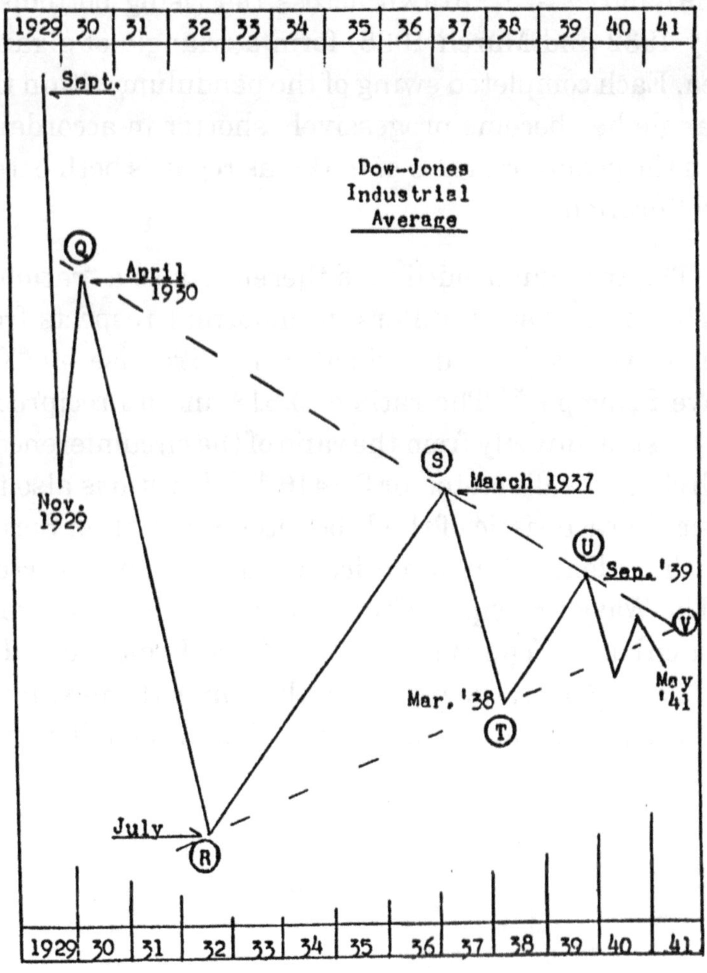

the greater the public interest and turnover in stocks, and vice versa. During recent years, the swings in the price trend have become progressively shorter, as is characteristic of movements within an orthodox triangle.

The swings of the Dow Jones Industrial monthly average, as shown in the accompanying chart, afford a clear explanation for this lack of confidence and resulting apathy. The two dashed lines, Ⓠ - Ⓥ (drawn across the falling tops of April 1930, March 1937, and September 1939) and Ⓡ - Ⓥ (drawn across the rising bottoms of July 1932 and March 1938) form a triangle of gigantic area. Each completed swing of the pendulum within this triangle has become progessively shorter in accordance with the geometric ratio of 0.618, as regards both extent and duration.

The triangular outline is therefore also a "ratio triangle," and as such, differs in important respects from the "wave triangle" described in my Treatise on "The Wave Principle."[3] The ratio of 0.618 and its reciprocal, 1.618, stem directly from the ratio of the circumference of a circle to the diameter, or 3.1416.[4] This ratio is also the basic characteristic of the Fibonacci Summation Series, which is identical in numerical count with the structure of The Wave Principle. This similarity is discussed fully in a circular, "The Basis of The Wave Principle."[5] The Fibonacci Series, the ratio of each term to the next term, and the reciprocal value, are revealed in the following:

Table of Relativity

First Term				Second Term	Ratio	Reciprocal Ratio
2	plus	3	equals	5	0.60	1.67
3		5		8	0.625	1.60
8		8		13	0.615	1.63
8		13		21	0.619	1.616
13		21		34	0.617	1.62
21		34		55	0.618	1.618
34		55		89	0.618	1.618
55		89		144	0.618	1.618

These ratios and series have been controlling and limiting the extent and duration of price trends, irrespective of wars, politics, production indices, the supply of money, general purchasing power, or other generally accepted methods of determining stock values. That this statement is true is verified by the following tabulation of important movements since April 1930:

The Cyclical Relativity of Market Trends

Wave	*Dates*		*Points*			
No.	*From*	*To*	*From*	*To*	*Change*	*Ratio*
R	Nov '28	Jul '32	296.0	40.5	255.5	
S	Jul '32	Mar '37	40.5	196.0	155.5	155.5 / 255.5 = 60.9%
T	Mar '37	Mar '38	196.0	97.0	99.0	99.0 / 155.5 = 63.6%
U	Mar '38	Sep '39	97.0	158.0	61.0	61.0 / 99.0 = 61.6%
						Avg. 62.0

Since the causes of this phenomenal market behavior originate in the relativity of the component cycles compressed within the triangular area, it is distinctly encouraging to be able to point out that the rapidly approaching apex of the triangle should mark the beginning of a relatively long period of increasing activity in the stock market.

R.N. Elliott

FOOTNOTES

[1] Copies of Educational Letters D through M are unavailable. However, a number of them were, as Elliott confirmed in a private letter to a client, included in their entirety in "Nature's Law," which is published in R.N. Elliott's Masterworks. A surviving record from the Library of Congress indicates that Educational Letter M was dated February 5, 1942 and entitled "Basic Elements of the Wave Principle."

[2] This treatise is an excellent innovative analysis and a correct conclusion.

[3] The difference Elliott points out is, in fact, crucial. Apparently a ratio triangle may appear apart from a wave triangle. Thus, the 13 year triangle is not a required interpretation despite the Fibonacci relationships. See Footnote 8 of Interpretive Letter 17.

[4] See discussion in the Precision Ratio Compass Manual (New Classics Library).

[5] The preceding Bulletin.

EDUCATIONAL BULLETIN N[1]

The Measurement of Mass Psychology

Webster's definition of psychology:

> "The traits, feelings, actions and attributes, collectively, of the mind."

In order to measure mass psychology, the action of the composite mind must be expressed in figures and plotted on a chart. When plotted, the resultant graph will show a pattern. These patterns follow definite rules. Many scientists have disclosed that human behavior (action of the composite mind) moves in waves, but they did not discover that these waves observe patterns, because graphed records were not then available.[2]

For years, the word "cycle" has been bandied about but never analyzed. The Wave Principle definitely describes the cycle of mass psychology. When plotting the fluctuations of human activity and spacing each entry at uniform periods of time, such as days, weeks, months or years, the result will be an "activity cycle," as shown in the diagram below. The letters across the top represent the months of the year, and the figures at the left represent the price or quantity.

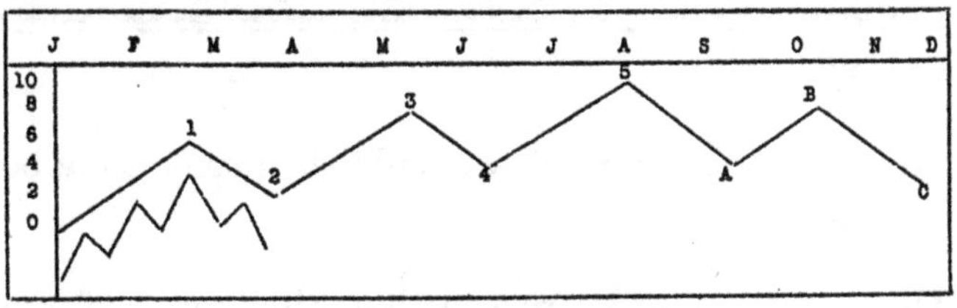

A cyclical pattern, or measurement of mass psychology, is 5 waves upward and 3 waves downward, total 8 waves. These patterns have forecasting value. When 5 waves upward have been completed, 3 waves down will follow, and vice versa.

There are several degrees of waves. For example, wave 1 shown in the above diagram may be composed of 5 minor waves, and wave 2 of 3 minor waves, all of lesser degree than the larger waves. The phenomenon described functions in every human activity that can be graphed, including stocks, bonds, volume, commodities, production, etc., etc. The above is a simple outline of a demonstrable fact.

Any device employed to predict the action of something else is unreliable. Opinion is invariably divided because it is based on different view points. It is humanly impossible for anyone to consolidate and correctly evaluate the effect when mixing war news, economics and politics.[3]

Prominent New York newspapers have seriously questioned the value of news as a market guide. News is never responsible for changes in the pattern of the activity cycle. *When market action agrees with news, it is simply a coincidence. When market action does not fit the news, it is quickly forgotten.*

Is it not time that you became acquainted with a simple Law of Nature that will guide you in any class of activity?

R.N. Elliott

FOOTNOTES

[1] Educational Bulletin N was published some time between March and September, 1942

[2] This is precisely the reason that Elliott was afforded the opportunity to discover the Wave Principle.

[3] This and the following paragraph are a wonderfully concise expression of a truth so basic and useful that, naturally, less than 1% of investors behave accordingly.

EDUCATIONAL BULLETIN O
The Future Pattern of the Market
October 26, 1942

The pattern of the past 21 years (1921-1942) furnishes a basis which may be used for forecasting that of the next 70 years, as well as estimating what the record may have been between 1776 and 1850.[1]

Graph 1 on the following page covers the entire period mentioned (1776-2012), and shows 5 waves of large degree. A Wave Principle cycle is always composed of 5 waves up and 3 waves down, regardless of the degree or size.

Waves 2 and 4 are always corrections. *Triangles may appear as wave 4, never as wave 2 insofar as I have observed.*[2] Therefore, the pattern of the period from 1929 to 1942, being a triangle, is wave Ⓘⓥ of a Supercycle.[3] Wave Ⓥ is about to start, and based on the duration of wave Ⓘⓘⓘ (1857-1929), it should terminate about the year 2012.[4]

Having established that wave Ⓘⓥ started in 1929, wave Ⓘⓘⓘ obviously ended in the same year. Wave Ⓘⓘⓘ of graph 1 is detailed in graph 2, from 1857 to 1929, using the Axe-Houghton Index.

The 5th wave of graph **2** started in 1896. It subdivided into 5 waves and its subdivided 5th wave, *starting in 1921, extended. Extensions never appear twice in a cycle.* Therefore, no extension of this degree should appear between 1942 and 2012.[5] Doubtless, neither did one appear in wave 1, previous to 1850, for which period I have no record. For these reasons, the two dashed lines in graph **1**,[6] previous to 1850 and following 1942, are sound conclusions.[7]

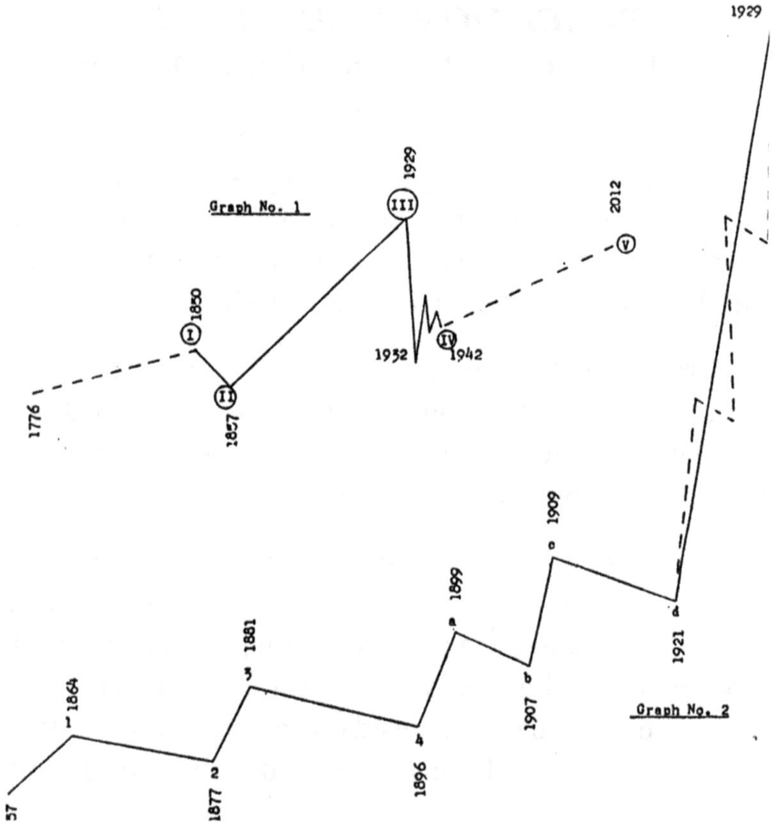

Economic History in the United States Previous to 1929

Previous to the middle of the 19th century, the ruling enterprise was farming, done by individuals, on a small scale with few, if any, hired employees. In the cities, commercial enterprise was largely subsidiary to the farm. Labor saving machinery, as we know it, was absent. On the farm and in the city, the "hired man" and the "boss" addressed each other by their first names and each was sympathetic with the other's problems. Time changed all this.

Natural resources, transportation and individual initiative are essential factors of progress.

In the development of the United States, the following natural resources were found in abundance: water power, coal, oil, metals, timber, etc. A temperate zone favored the production of almost every item of food and clothing. Two oceans and two friendly neighbors created ideal geographical boundaries on all sides.

Transportation came gradually: Barge canals, the pony express, steamboats, railroads, automobiles and airplanes.

These blessings were extensive and required immense capital for development. This could be supplied only through corporations, financed by private capital in exchange for securities in quantities to suit the public. Managements were shifted occasionally, and these circumstances gradually opened a breach between employee and employer. Management oftentimes became autocratic and ruthless towards owners, employees, the public and each other.

During the 1890s, the pendulum began to swing in the opposite direction. Labor formed unions for self protection. Political candidates joined hands with labor. Managerial and financial domination culminated during the 1920s. (See graph **2**).

Wave Ⓥ of Graph **1** will embrace three bull markets and two intervening bear markets. The amplitude of waves (percentagewise) and volume will resemble those of the period between 1857 and 1909, as depicted in graph **2**. No one now living will witness a "New Era" of the 1920s type.[8]

R.N. Elliott

FOOTNOTES

[1] Elliott's entire analysis here is a repeat of the analysis in Interpretive Letter No. 17, updated at a time when he was certain that the market had passed its Supercycle wave (IV). bottom. The overall analysis remains a remarkable feat, and was shown to be correct with the new availability of past data, as presented in *Elliott Wave Principle*. Also see Footnote 7 below and Footnote 2 with Interpretive Letter No. 17.

[2] While Elliott's *Financial World* articles addressed this idea, this is the first definite formulation of this guideline. See Footnote 6 of Interpretive letter No. 27.

[3] Should read "Grand Supercycle."

[4] See Footnote 13 of Interpretive Letter 17.

[5] Elliott's example suggests that within a five wave structure, only one subwave will contain an extension in one of its impulse subwaves, whereas actually the correct guideline is that only one impulse wave within a five wave structure will be an extension. There is no reason why an extension should not appear as a *subwave* of each impulse wave in a five wave sequence. In fact, it nearly always does. As history has born out, the rise from 1942 to 1966 was an extended wave. However, if Wave (III) *was* an extension, wave (I) and (V) should *not* be.

[6] Elliott was sometimes careless with his drawings. Wave (V) in graph **1**, for instance, was clearly intended to climb to a new high. Neither did the 1932 low fall below the peak of wave (I).

[7] Elliott's historical wave count is brilliant and accurate. His conclusion, made only six months after the 1942 low, was entirely correct that that low would not be exceeded on the downside prior to a multi-decade advance. His conclusion regarding the rise into the beginning of his data in 1850 was similarly accurate, although the actual orthodox top of wave (I) occurred in 1836 and the preceding low in 1784.

[8] Whether he means a wave V of Ⓘⓘⓘ or a six times multiple in eight years, he was correct. However, the fifth wave of Cycle degree which occurred in the 1980s provided similar "New Era" characteristics, and was analogous at the Supercycle, though not the Grand Supercycle, degree. Even so, very few people living during the 1920s were around to witness it.

EDUCATIONAL BULLETIN P
Index of Psychology
April 1938 to February 1943

In Confidential Letters of September 18, 1942[1] and previous dates, it is stated that bear market endings have a tendency to "fray out," that is, fail to entirely complete their patterns.[2]

A new index, mentioned in Interpretive Letter No. 24, solves the problem.

On the next page will be found two graphs covering the period from April 1938 to February 1943.

Graph **Y** represents the Dow Jones Industrial Average. Interpretive Letter No. 26 shows that wave ④ of the 13-year triangle ended in October 1939. Therefore, wave ④ started at that point.

Wave ⑤ is a "flat."[3] Wave A is composed of 3 Minor waves, a, b and c, down to May, 1940. Wave B is composed of 3 Minor waves, a, b and c, upward to November 1940. Wave C started November 1940 and was to be composed of 5 Minor waves, 1, 2, 3, 4 and 5.[4] Minor waves 1, 2 and 3 developed and ended in April 1942. Minor wave 4 was to be composed of 3 minute waves up to October 13, 1942. Instead of 3 waves upward, 5 waves developed, ending in February 1943.

Therefore, the 5 wave movement from April 1942 to February becomes Primary wave 1 of the ensuing bull market.

Graph **Z** portrays the new index to which I have given the name "Psychology."[5] As will be noted, the

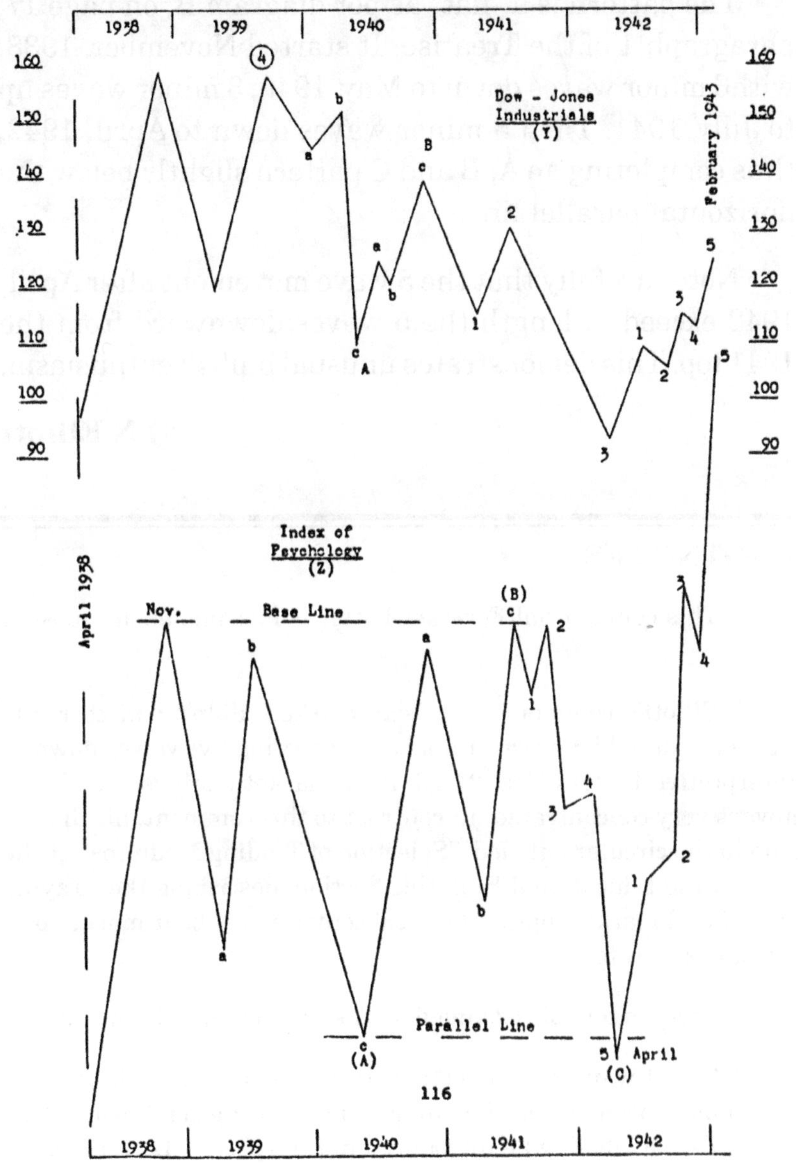

pattern differs from that presented in Graph **Y**.[6] Note that the tops from November 1938 to July 1941 describe a horizontal base line.

The pattern is a "flat" as per diagram B, on page 17, paragraph 1 of the Treatise. It started November, 1938, with6 minor waves down to May, 1940, 3 minor waves up to July, 1941. Then 5 minor waves down to April, 1942, thus completing an A, B and C pattern slightly below the horizontal parallel line.

Note carefully that the 5 wave movement after April, 1942 exceed in length the 5 waves downward from the 1941 top. This demonstrates unusual bullish enthusiasm.

R.N.Elliott

FOOTNOTES

[1] This confidential Forecast Letter is missing, as are most of them.

[2] Elliott's comment that bear markets didn't end correctly was a result of his incorrect analysis expecting five waves down in Interpretive Letters Nos. 24-26. Bear market endings are almost always very concentrated. In contrast to this comment, his discussion in the circular entitled, "Selection of Trading Mediums" at the start of the Educational Bulletins Section, describing the "fraying out" of bull market tops and the concentration of bear market bottoms, is accurate.

[3] This is a terrible looking flat. The one in graph **Z** is a real one.

[4] Elliott wanted a corrective structure for a triangle leg, but would have been better off calling it a double zigzag, labeled A-B-C-X-A-B-C, a labeling he introduced in Interpretive Letter No. 12. He would then have avoided having to say that the expected Minor waves 4 and 5 failed to develop. Still, however, the best count for the 1937-1942 decline is an Ⓐ - Ⓑ - Ⓒ, with a triangle for wave Ⓑ, as shown in the accompanying chart.

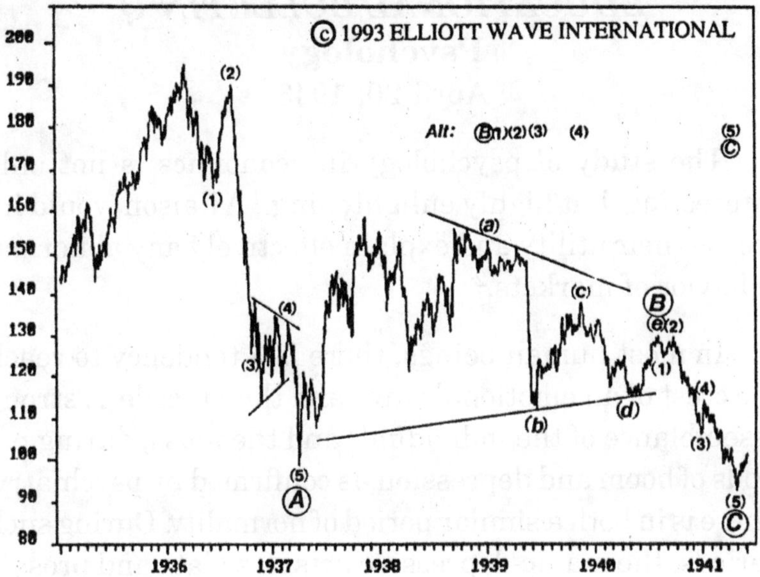

5 The index was first illustrated, without this title, as graph Y in Interpretive Letter No. 24. It is referenced again in Interpretive Letter No. 34.

6 Though clearly a useful tool, one reason why Elliott developed this index may have been to have some measure of market prices which showed a higher low in 1942 as compared to that of 1938, thus making it consistent with the concept of a triangle. The use of the word "psychology" is probably due to his reading Pigou (see Educational Bulletin Q).

EDUCATIONAL BULLETIN Q

Psychology

April 20, 1943

The study of psychology in economics is not only interesting, but highly enlightening.[1] A liaison would increase their utility and explain effectively any abnormal behavior of markets.[2]

In most human beings, there is a tendency to reach the crest of an emotional wave and then recede. A strong resemblance of the individual[3] and the mass, during periods of boom and depression, is confirmed by psychiatry. There is in both a similar period of normality. During such periods, the manic-depressive acts in sedate and prosaic manner. During the exaltation period, his mental activity is very great indeed. He rushes about creating, planning and writing. After reaching the crisis in his exaltation, he starts on a downward wave of the depressive phase. The downward trend begins with a slight loss of confidence, develops into a condition of anxiety and ends with utter despair concerning the future. This completes the cycle, and from this point on, confidence and poise are gradually regained.[4]

How far booms and depressions are due to purely economic events or to exaggeration of temperament would be hard to define, of course. Yet there is more to it than, at first thought, one might suppose.

The French economist, Pigou,[5] has discussed at length psychological errors and their relation to booms and depression. He maintains that an error of optimism tends to create, throughout the community, a certain measure of psychological interdependence6 until it leads to a crisis. Then the error of optimism dies and gives birth to an error of pessimism.

The point I wish to make is that these phenomena occur with great regularity in business cycles as well as the cycle of a manic-depressive. All humans seem to be subject to varying moods. This is particularly noticeable in the United States.

A barometer gives warning of impending change not yet evidenced. I have developed a stock market barometer of Mass Economic Psychology. It gives warning, months in advance, of impending change and indicates points of reversal. It is not a Price Index, such as the Dow Jones Industrials, nevertheless stock market records are employed.[7]

For the first time in six years the following indices are "in gear",[8] as defined by The Wave Principle:

New York:	***London:***
Industrials,	Industrials,
Rails,	Rails.
Utilities,	Corporate Bonds.

R.N. Elliott

FOOTNOTES

[1] Economics is properly a branch of sociology, although few understand that to be the case.

[2] He appears to mean behavior that economists cannot figure out or predict, which is, of course, to say, normal market behavior.

[3] He means to say, "the manic-depressive individual."

[4] This model is a good one. Social mood swings are pathological. Most individuals' mood swings are not. Manic- depressives are people whose pathology is the same as society's. They are viewed as ill because 1) their mood swings are predictable and 2) they occur regardless of specific outside stimuli. The Wave Principle reveals that social mood swings have these same characteristics.

[5] It is probable that Collins introduced Elliott to the ideas of Pigou.

[6] The key error is individual dependence upon the ideas of others. Independent thinkers can recognize the social error.

[7] Interpretive Letter No. 34 later refers to the index as equivalent to today's NYSE stock index. For further discussion, see Educational Bulletin P.

[8] This observation was made one year into a 24 year bull market.

EDUCATIONAL BULLETIN S[1]
Cyclical Periodicities
May 25, 1943

1. Interest in cycles is increasing rapidly. A non-profit "Foundation for the Study of Cycles" is located at 400 West 118th St., New York City.[2] The Committee is composed of prominent educators of Great Britain, Canada and the United States. An article by its Director, Mr. Edward R. Dewey, in *Science Digest* for April 1943 entitled "The Future Foretold by Cycles" is a reprint of a broadcast given at the invitation of the General Electric Co. I suggest that you ask him to send you his brochure on "Cycles" and bulletin entitled "Awards for 1943." The Foundation merits enthusiastic support.

2. In the same magazine, on page 33, may be found an article by two physicians. The third paragraph reads as follows:

> "This life is vastly more complex than the orbs of earth and sun, but like the heavenly bodies, the human life cycle is governed by natural laws. In surety and precision, the laws of development are comparable to those of gravitation".

In the *Science Digest* for May 1943 appears an article entitled "Rhythms indicate early Peace." It describes the results of research by the University of Kansas and is very impressive.

3. The brochure issued by the Foundation mentions graphs and describes periodicities between peaks and valleys of many items, such as epidemics of influenza and pneumonia, production of lynx pelts, tent caterpillars, salmon, etc. The periodicities described are fairly uniform between peaks and valleys of each item.

4. After many years of research, I developed the idea that the series of numbers listed below comprises nature's law of human activities, both Periodicities and Waves:

3 5 8 13 21 34 55 89 144.

The sum of any two adjoining numbers equals the next higher number. For example, 5 plus 8 equals 13. Each number is approximately .618 of the next higher number.

A few examples of Periodicities of the stock market between major tops and bottoms are given below:

From	*To*	*Periodicities*
1921	1929	8 years
September 1929	July 1932	34 months
1929	1937	8 years
1932	1937	5 years
March 1937	April 1942	5 years
March 1937	March 1938	13 months
April 1942	May 1943	13 months

5. The market makes wave patterns continuously, all of which are described in my Treatise entitled "The Wave Principle."

6. A complete cycle employs all of the serial numbers listed in paragraph 4. They repeat as follows:

	Number of Waves in a		
	Bull Market	*Bear Market*	*Complete Cycle*
Primaries	5	3	8
Intermediates	21	13	34
Minors	89	55	144

In financial activities, cycles are not uniformly spaced, but Periodicities and Waves correlate. The ratio .618 mentioned in paragraph 4 is frequently useful.

7. Recently, I developed a barometer that gives ample warning of approaching reversal of psychology.

8. Copies of this circular will be sent to anyone you suggest. Inquiries are invited.

R.N. Elliott

FOOTNOTES

[1] Educational Bulletin R is missing from this collection.

[2] Their current address is The Foundation for the Study of Cycles, 2600 Michelson Dr., Suite 1570, Irvine, CA 92715-1607.

EDUCATIONAL BULLETIN T
Patents, Stocks and Temperature
September 9, 1943

On the next page are shown two series of graphs for the period, 1850-1942. The upper series **X** represents the yearly number of applications for patents. The lower series **Z** represents stocks. Upward to 1929, both present the same pattern, 5 waves, *of which the 5th extended*, as diagramed with paragraph 3 on page 17 of my Treatise entitled "The Wave Principle."

Politics, wars, finance, economics and the stock market are tinged with emotion and mass psychology, whereas patents are not. The success or failure of an invention is never due to the date of discovery[1] or the number of inventions and inventors at any particular time.

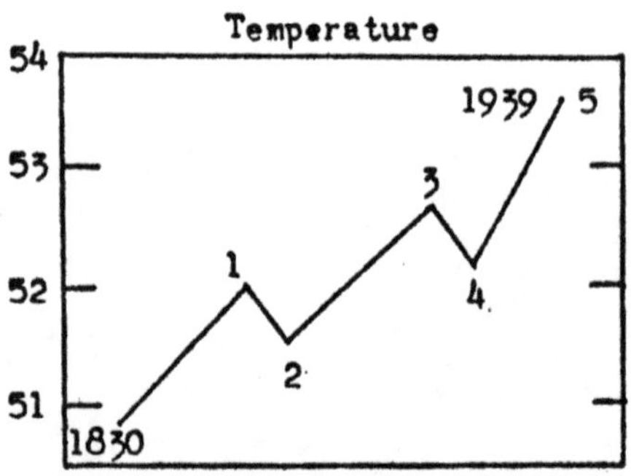

The next graph portrays the mean temperature by decades in New York City over a period of 110 years, in 5 waves.

The three subjects mentioned, patents, stocks and temperature, are totally different in character:

Temperature – not a human activity,
Stocks – an emotional human activity,
Patents – a human activity but not emotional.[2]

This demonstrates a Law of Nature in diverse activities.

Graph **X1** below is the outline of patents from 1850 to 1929. *The 5th wave extended* and its details are shown in **X2**, also 5 waves.

Graph **Z1** is the outline of stocks from 1857 to 1929. *The 5th wave extended,*[3] and details are shown in graph **Z2**.

The 5th wave of **Z2** is detailed in graph **Z3**. The 5th wave of **Z3** extended in the same manner.

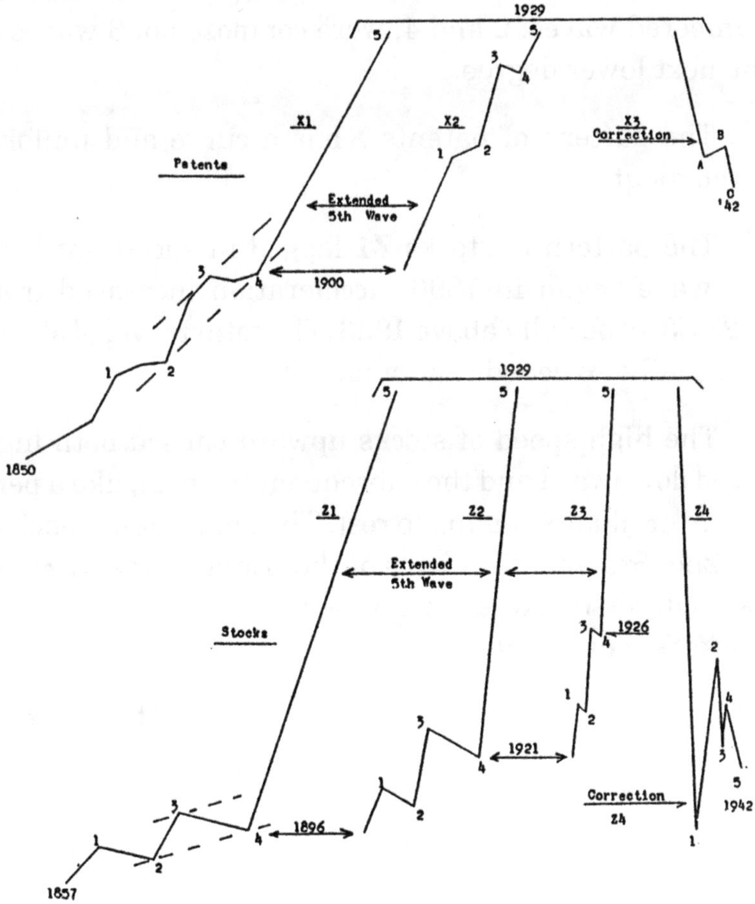

Graph **X3** is the correction of **X1**, in 3 waves, A, B and C to 1942.

Graph **Z4** is the correction of **Z1**, and the pattern is a triangle to 1942.

All of the above patterns are diagramed in my Treatise.

All of the odd numbered waves, 1, 3 and 5, were composed of 5 waves of the next lower degree; all of the even numbered waves, 2 and 4, were composed of 3 waves of the next lower degree.

The pattern of patents **X1** is a curve and uniform throughout.

The pattern of stocks **Z1** lagged in speed until the 5th wave began in 1896. Acceleration increased from 1921 **Z3**, especially above 1926. The total travel of stocks eventually exceeded that of patents.

The high speed of stocks upward caused both high speed downward and the subsequent triangle, like a pendulum gradually coming to rest. The amplitude of each of the 2nd, 3rd and 4th waves of the triangle was 61.8% of its predecessor. Note the mathematical precision of the market's movements.

R.N. Elliott

FOOTNOTES

[1] Perhaps not to the date per se, but certainly the ease of mention is determined substantially by the culture and the "times," since success depends upon actions taken by many other human beings. Elliott says as much in the first paragraph of Educational Bulletin X. See also Footnote 3 below.

[2] To the contrary, it is my contention that net human achievement is greatly a function of the state and trend of social and cultural psychology.

[3] The similarity in the two charts is an extremely important observation, precisely because it suggests that patents are tied in with the emotional state of a society as reflected by the wave structure of its stock market. Besides providing an emotional environment conducive to production and invention, of course, a rising stock market also provides an environment of prosperity, and thus extra capital for new ventures and extra spare time for inventors.

EDUCATIONAL BULLETIN U

Inflation

September 20, 1943

The moment is opportune to demonstrate the utility of The Wave Principle during inflation of stocks, commodities, etc. The general public is concerned about inflation of the necessities of life, and investors are interested in inflation of securities. Commodities and stock do not, necessarily, inflate in unison.[1]

The all important feature is to be able to recognize inflation, if and when it starts, and, when it terminates.

....

An advance is composed of 5 waves. Ordinarily, a correction (a, b and c) penetrates the base line as shown in diagram **V** (next page).

Graph **W** shows the same pattern except that the correction (a, b and c) does not penetrate the base line, and therefore indicates inflation.

Graph **X** shows the Dow Jones Industrial average during the inflationary period, 1921 to 1929. Corrections did not penetrate base lines and the entire movement presented a quarter-circle curve. Note the dashed outline.

Graph **Z** represents the London Industrial index from 1940 to date. Five waves upward were completed on January 29, 1943. From that date to June 15, 1943, a correction (a, b and c) moved in 3 shallow waves, sidewise, without penetrating the base line, and from June 15 the advance was resumed. This indicates inflation.

....

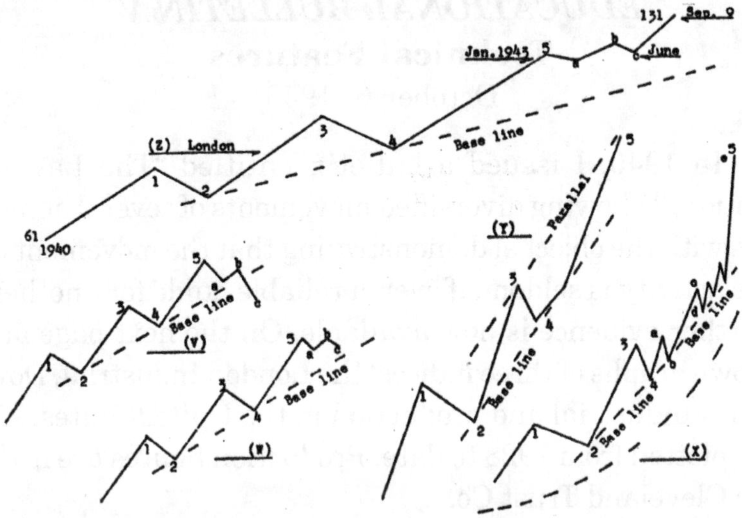

Termination of inflation is indicated by two methods which coincide:

(a) The 5th wave completes its extension and the entire movement presents a curve, as in graph **X**, which is plotted on *arithmetic* scale.

(b) When the same index is plotted on *logarithmic* scale, the curve is eliminated and the entire movement of 5 waves, including extension, is confined within one channel, as outlined in graph **Y** and in detail on page 38 of my Treatise.

R.N. Elliott

FOOTNOTE

[1] Both in this discussion and in Chapter XII of "Nature's Law," Elliott indicates that by "inflation," he means a persistent, steady increase in price on a percentage basis with minimal pull-backs along the way. In that context, the discussion is accurate, unlike the comments in the Forecast Letter of March 7, 1945 (see Footnote 3 thereof).

EDUCATIONAL BULLETIN V

Technical Features

October 6, 1943

In 1940, I issued a bulletin entitled "The Law of Motion,"[1] showing diversified movements of several activities with the object of demonstrating that the movement of one activity is seldom, if ever, a reliable guide for another. Further evidence is now available. On the next page are shown graphs of three indices, the London Industrial, Dow Jones Industrial and production in the United States. All are plotted from 1928 to date. Production figures are from the Cleveland Trust Co.

Graph ***Y***: The Dow Jones Industrials registered a 5 wave triangle from November 1928 (the orthodox top) to April 1942. The term "orthodox" is described in my Treatise. The amplitude of each of the 2nd, 3rd and 4th waves of the triangle to its predecessor is approximately 61.8%. The existence of the triangle is proved by (a) its outline, (b) the time element, (c) the composition of each wave, and (d) the uniform ratio of each wave to its predecessor. High speed inflation from 1921 to 1929 (8 years) caused the rapid decline to 1932. These, in turn, caused the triangle, *which simulates a pendulum coming to rest*. (See Treatise, page 21, paragraph 3, type "C", "Symmetrical Triangle.") The triangle disregarded the following events which occurred during its 13-year period:

reversal from Republican to New Deal administrations,
devaluation of the dollar,
repudiation of the gold clause in government bonds,
two-term precedent shattered,

the 2nd World War started in 1939,
the production index started upward in 1938 and
finished its pattern of 5 waves in June 1941.

*Graph **X***: The London Industrials registered tops in June 1929 at 140 and in December 1936 at 143. The lows in 1932 and 1940 were the same, 61. From 1940, they advanced to 131 and are now within 12 points of the 1936 high. It is said that England has reversed from a creditor to a debtor nation. London stocks invaded the stratosphere in 1720, 1815 and 1899, but not in 1929.

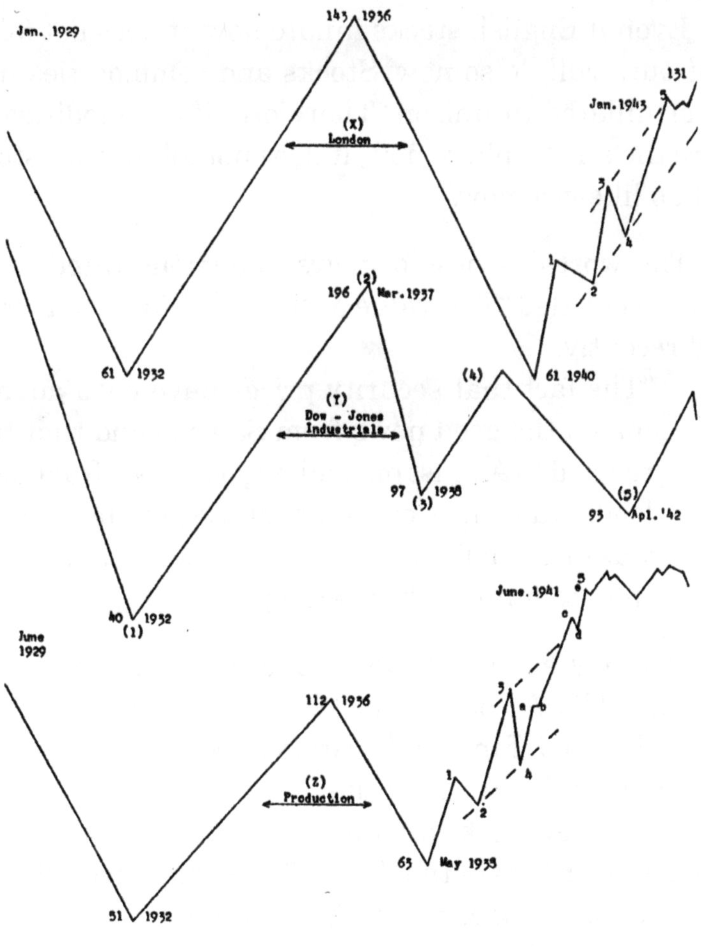

Graph **Z**: The production index registered tops in June 1929 at 116 and in 1936 at 112, and a low in 1938 at 63. From 63, a complete advance of 5 waves finished its pattern in June 1941, before the D-J Industrials started up from the end of their triangle in April 1942.

During the period from 1857 to 1929, we participated in 3 wars, Civil, Spanish and World War I; nevertheless, the pattern of the Supercycle movement was perfect, as demonstrated in a recent bulletin entitled "Patents, Stocks and Temperature."

Even if English stocks inflate now, it does not follow that ours will do so now. Stocks and commodities have never inflated in unison. Therefore, if commodities explore the stratosphere now, it does not follow that stocks will do likewise now.

The worthlessness of news is demonstrated in my bulletin entitled "The Value of News."[2] A financial writer said recently:

> "The fact that security prices have been advancing on the good news from Salerno and that they reacted in August on similar good news from Sicily leads students to conclude that the August reaction was due chiefly to technical considerations rather than to military happenings."

One day about two years ago, London experienced a severe "blitz." London stocks advanced and New York stocks declined. Financial writers in both places stressed the "blitz" as the cause. At the time, London was in an up trend and New York in a down trend. Each followed its pattern regardless of the "blitz." The same wave behavior occurred following Mussolini's exit, July 25.

The above analysis proves that technical features govern the market at ALL times.[3]

R.N. Elliott

FOOTNOTES

[1] I.e., Educational Bulletin C. See also Educational Bulletin B, entitled "Cycles," and the accompanying footnotes.

[2] This is one of the missing Educational Bulletins, although a section by the same name was included in "Nature's Law" (see *R.N. Elliott's Masterworks*).

[3] This simple statement is true and very profound.

EDUCATIONAL BULLETIN W
Gold
November 1, 1943

The graphs on the next page are of special interest due to the nature of the subject, the price of gold, and the remarkably long period, seven centuries, covered by ONE pattern. All details are in accordance with diagrams described in my Treatise on The Wave Principle.

The Lower Graph was published by the London *Economist* of November 16, 1935 on page 970, showing the market value in English shillings per fine ounce of gold during 685 years, from 1250 to 1935, and plotted on *arithmetic* scale.

As will be noted in paragraph 2 on page 17 of my Treatise, only one of the three advancing waves, 1, 3, or 5, will extend. Extended waves are composed of 9 waves of the next lower degree, as diagramed in paragraph 3 on page 17. Wave ③ extended (waves a to i); therefore, wave ⑤ will not extend.

"Double retracement" of extensions is described and graphed on pages 17 and 18 of my Treatise. The extended portion of wave 3 was "double-retraced" by waves ④ and ⑤.[1]

Corrective waves 2 and 4 are usually dissimilar; that is, one is small and the other large, or better said, "simple" or "complex."[2] In this graph, wave (2) is "simple" and wave (4) is "complex." Note the letters (A), (B) and (C)[3] of wave ④.

Underlined numbers are years; encircled are waves; others are shillings. Upper graph is *logarithmic* scale, lower graph is *arithmetic* scale.

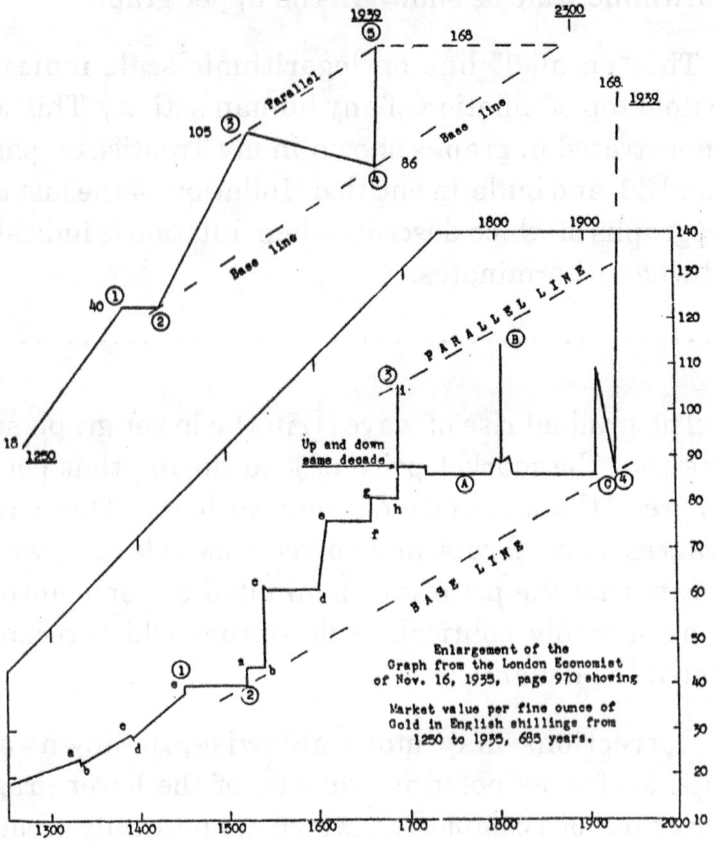

The utility of "base" and "parallel" lines, forming a channel, are described in my Treatise. In this arithmetically plotted graph, the "parallel" line intersects the price line at 133.

When this graph was published by the *Economist* in 1935, wave ⑤ had reached 140 shillings. From 1935 to 1939, wave ⑤ advanced to 168 where it is now (November 1943).

When an advance of 5 waves is completed within the channel on *arithmetic* scale, there is no inflation.

The Upper Graph: When the price line exceeded 133, inflation was indicated and necessitated employment of logarithmic scale as shown in the upper graph.

The "parallel" line on logarithmic scale indicates the final top of inflation of any human activity. This was demonstrated in graphs shown in my Treatise on pages 37 and 38, and bulletin entitled "Inflation,"4 the last two paragraphs of which describe when inflation is indicated and when it terminates.

....

The gradual rise of wave ① in the lower graph suggests that the market price of gold during that period was "free," that is, not fixed by any authority. Thereafter, advances were abrupt and corrections sidewise, which indicate that the price was dominated by some authority, presumably political, such as that which recently inflated the dollar.

Corrections may move sidewise, or downward and sidewise, as noted in wave ④ of the lower graph. Corrections of a completed pattern are naturally greater, in time and/or price, than any correction *within* the pattern.[5]

Under the law described by the Wave Principle, when a pattern has been completed, as indicated in the upper graph by the contact of wave ⑤ with the "parallel" line, no further advance in price will occur until *after* the price line has penetrated the "base" line at some point.

Therefore, the probability is that the present price of gold, 168 shillings, will remain stationary *at least* until it contacts the "base line" about the year 2300, as indicated by the junction of the dashed lines at the extreme right of the upper graph.[6]

As the laws described by The Wave Principle have been observed for seven centuries, there is every reason to expect that they will continue in force indefinitely.

R.N. Elliott

FOOTNOTES

[1] Regardless of Elliott's listing of double retracement as a separate guideline, it would always occur in the natural development of prices as they follow the Wave Principle.

[2] See Interpretive Letter No. 27 and Footnote 7 thereof.

[3] Showed in circles on the graph.

[4] I.e., Educational Bulletin U.

[5] This statement is a good guide to the "right look" and a correct count.

[6] The conclusion from all this analysis was erroneous. If Elliott had understood that third waves usually exhibit acceleration and extension, the steepness of wave ⑤ on both charts would have been a tipoff that a third wave extension was in progress. (See Footnote 1 of Interpretive Letter No. 13.) In the lower chart, Elliott's Ⓐ and Ⓑ waves are probably better labeled ④ and ⑤, thus completing a large first wave. The second wave corrected back to the previous fourth, as is typical, and a multi-century third wave rise then commenced.

Autocracy and Bureaucracy[1]

December 13, 1943

This is a story of two periods, *before* and *after* 1906.

1st Period: In the early days, farming was the principal occupation. Here and there, a farmer might own a store or manufacture something, as a sideline. Manufacturing was on a piece-work plan and performed in the home. Employees and employers were familiar with each others' affairs and called one another by their first names.

Patents and the introduction of machinery gradually changed everything. Factories became necessary and required capital. Partnerships, then corporations followed. Foremen, supervisors and managers came as a consequence. The former familiarity between employee and employer disappeared and was not replaced by intimacy between worker and foreman. When employers brought pressure to bear on foremen for greater and better production, the foremen knew only one way to accomplish results, and it was not the right way.

The "Louisiana Purchase," conquest of California, acquisition of Texas and Oregon, together with settlement of boundaries with Mexico and Canada, added a large and immensely valuable territory. Then came the "Iron Horse." The Civil War settled a long and perplexing problem.

The "corporation" provided funds for building railroads to connect the vast territory. Corporation management became arrogant with the public, political sub-divisions and each other.

Corporate management dominated politicians with "free passes" and other "favors." Employees were browbeaten. The Southern Pacific, under Huntington, controlled the State of California. The stranglehold was broken by Senator Hiram W. Johnson when he was Governor of that State.[2]

These conditions developed new methods of abuse which were "awful but lawful," such as railroad "rate wars," railroad tariffs based on "all the traffic will bear," employees working 10 and 12 hours a day without vacations, "bucket shops," and manipulation of stocks on the exchanges.

In order to form an idea of practices then in vogue, it is suggested that the following books be read:

The History of the Standard Oil Co, by Ida M. Tarbell,
The Octopus, by Frank Norris,
The Jungle and *Oil*, by Upton Sinclair.

2nd Period: The tide turned in 1906 when President Theodore Roosevelt signed the Hepburn Act, which empowered the I.C.C. to control the railroads. The results have been very beneficial[3] and possibly quite difficult for the present generation to appreciate. It may be said that the Hepburn Act was the beginning of Bureaucracy. I recommend reading an article entitled "The Dead Hand of Bureaucracy," which appeared in the *Reader's Digest* for October 1940.

With the passage of the Hepburn Act, politicians and labor leaders joined hands. Labor Unions became general. Certainly they have done an immense amount of good because employers were compelled to treat employes as human beings. Personnel managers are becoming popular and are necessary.

Autocracy moved the pendulum upward to its zenith in 1906. Bureaucracy reversed the pendulum and reached it zenith in 1940 when John L. Lewis opposed the reelection of Mr. Roosevelt whose labor policy was simply the culmination of reaction to Autocracy of the First Period. From 1906 to 1940, 34 years elapsed.[4]

R.N. Elliott

FOOTNOTES

[1] This is an additional circular.

[2] As a former railroad accountant, Elliott must have had some experience with these events and conditions. On the other hand, he seems to have been motivated to write these paragraphs after reading the four revisionist anti-industry books next listed.

[3] This clause and much of the discussion contrasts starkly with Elliott's observation in Interpretive Letter No. 23 that the peak relative valuation for the Rails occured in the same year that the I.C.C. was created. Here he seems to be saying that despite the decimation of the industry and its profits, there were great benefits to labor, a logic which can only be carried so far before it collapses.

[4] Elliott's larger point is that all trends go "too far," and that the initial reaction to its extreme is beneficial. Then that new trend ultimately goes "too far," and the pattern repeats, continually self-adjusting and ultimately resulting in progress. The periods of each pendulum swing, he implies, are tied to the Fibonacci sequence.

EDUCATIONAL BULLETIN X

Nature's Law

January 6, 1944

"Let imagination remind you how all the varied present does but repeat the past and rehearse the future."

Marcus Aurelius (120 - 180 A.D.)

Progress is measured by the development of new ideas. Frequently, a good idea must await developments in other fields. For example, the new ideas of the Wright Brothers would have been useless without the internal combustion motor. The daily high-low range of stock averages facilitated my discovery of the patterns of human activity.

The earliest record that I have been able to find of the Key to "The Wave Principle" is the Great Pyramid of Egypt, which was constructed about 40 centuries ago. The original dimensions of this pyramid are estimated to have been: base 756 feet square, 481 feet high. The ratio is .636. A pyramid presents 5 surfaces and 8 lines. The ratio of these numbers is .625. These numbers and their ratio are basic in Nature's Law.

When Pythagoras (Greek philosopher 500 B.C.) returned from a visit to Egypt, he diagramed a pyramid and underlined it with the cryptic inscription, "Key to the Secret of the Universe." History demonstrates that the contributions of the Greeks to structural design were artistic and symmetrical.

Mr. Jay Hambidge spent many years researching the records of Greek art and wrote a book entitled *Practical Applications of Dynamic Symmetry*. One of the chapters is entitled "The Law of Phyllotaxis" (the system or order of leaf arrangement). A copy of pages 27 and 28 is attached hereto. Mr. Hambidge demonstrates that Greek art is based on a "Summation Series." Fibonacci, an Italian mathematician of the 13th century, disclosed this series.

Mr. Hambidge was an artist and confined his discussion to symmetrical design and leaf arrangement. I recommend a careful review of his book.

My discoveries disclose that the human body, human activity, time, music, color, etc., follow the same Law of Nature, as they conform to the Fibonacci mathematical Summation Series, the universal Key, which lends importance and authenticity.

My bulletin of October 1, 1940, entitled "The Basis of The Wave Principle," cites as references Pythagoras, Fibonacci, Hambidge, et al.

Inquiries are invited.

When discussing the researches of Sir William Beveridge, the noted British economist, the *London Economist* said editorially:

> "Sir William's researches have emphasized once again that the more the trade cycle is studied, the more it seems to follow the pressure of forces which, if they are not wholly beyond the reach of human control, have at least enough of the inexorable in their nature to make the policies of government resemble the struggle of fish caught in the tides. He might have added that it overrides economic policies."

R.N. Elliott

From

Practical Applications of Dynamic Symmetry,

by Jay Hambidge. Pages 27 and 28 are reproduced by courtesy of Yale University Press.

Botanists use the disk of the sunflower as a sort of general illustration of the law of leaf arrangement. It exhibits the phenomenon in nearly two-dimensional form.

The seeds are distributed over the sunflower disk in rhomboidal shaped sockets and the complex of these sockets forms a design of intersecting curves, the pattern being something like the old fashioned chasing on watchcases.

This pattern of curves is the interesting feature of the sunflower seed arrangement.

First. The curve itself is a definite kind of curve. As a matter of fact it is quite like the curve of shell growth. It is regular and possesses certain mathematical properties. These properties are a necessary consequence of uniform growth, as will be explained presently.

Second. When these curves are counted, it will be found that a normal sunflower disk of five or six inches in diameter has 89. Winding in one direction there are 55, and in the other direction there are 34. That is to say, the normal head exhibits 55 curves crossing 34. The two numbers are written 34 + 55. Below the apex flower of the stalk, there are usually secondary flowers, smaller in size. The curve-crossing numbers for these are generally 21 + 34. Lower on the stalk may be tertiary flowers of late development. The curve-crossing numbers of these are 13 + 21.

At Oxford, in England, sunflowers have been nourished to produce abnormal disks, and the curve-crossing numbers have increased from 34 + 55 to 55 + 89. Professor Arthur H. Church, a leading modern authority on this fascinating subject, tells us of a gigantic disk raised at Oxford whereon the curve-crossing numbers were 89 + 144.

Around the seed complex of the flower disk there is an arrangement of florets. Like the seeds, these exhibit curve-crossing numbers. They are usually 5 + 8.

If we begin at the bottom of the plant stalk and count the actual number of leaves up to the flower disk, we are likely to find, as we wind our progress around the stalk, that we pass a certain number of leaves before we find one imposed directly over the one first counted, and that this number and the number of revolutions about the stalk, are constant between each leaf imposition. These will represent curve-crossing numbers belonging to the same series of numbers exhibited by the seeds and florets.

The numbers we have mentioned belong to what is called a summation series, so called because each number represents a sum of preceding numbers of the series, in this case 2.

This series of numbers is: 1, 2, 3, 5, 8, 13, 21, 34, 55, 89, 144, etc.

Each member of this series is obtained by adding together two preceding numbers. If we take any two members of this series and divide one into the other as, say, 34 into 55, we obtain a ratio, and this ratio is constant throughout the series; that is to say, any lesser number divided into any greater number which immediately succeeds it produces the same ratio. This ratio is 1.618 plus, a number with a never ending fraction.

If we reverse the operation and divide 55 into 34, we obtain the number .618 plus. It will be noticed that the difference between these two results is 1, or unity. It will also be noticed that when we make these two divisional operations that there is a slight error. This is due to the fact that the series is not quite accurate when expressed in whole numbers. There should be a very small fraction. But as the error is within that of observation in the growing plant, the whole number is retained to facilitate checking.

It is an extraordinary coincidence that this ratio of 1.618 or .618 is a ratio which fascinated the ancient Greeks exceedingly. Extraordinary, because they could have had no suspicion that it was connected with the architecture of plants. It was called by them extreme and mean ratio. During the Middle Ages, it was given the name Divine Section, and in fairly recent time, Golden Section.

EDUCATIONAL BULLETIN Y
Dynamic Symmetry
February 14, 1944

Dynamic Symmetry is a Law of Nature, and therefore the basis of all form and activity, including cycles and patterns in the stock market.

Dictionary definitions of the word "Cycle":

A period of time.
An entire turn or circle.
A spiral leaf structure.
A series that repeats itself.

Since the discovery that the Earth is round, the cycle has been the subject of much research. There are 3 classes of cycles:

(A) Uniform periodicities between peaks and between nadirs, such as day and night, seasons of the year, tides, epidemics, weather, and swarms of insects. The reader may be interested in an article by Donald G. Cooley entitled "Cycles Predict the Future," published in *Mechanix Illustrated* in its issue for February 1944.

(B) Periodicities caused by variable astronomical aspects.[1]

(C) Patterns, Time and Ratio, in accordance with a summation series disclosed by Fibonacci, an Italian mathematician of the 13th century. The series is repeated herewith:

1 - 2 - 3 - 5 - 8 - 13 - 13 - 21 - 34 - 55 - 89 - 144.

This series functions in numerous fields, for example:

(1) Mechanical Laws. Mr. A. H. Church is the author of a very interesting book entitled "The Relation of Phyllotaxis to Mechanical Laws."

(2) Phyllotaxis, or leaf arrangement of plants. Mr. Jay Hambidge spent many years researching the records of Greek art, and is the author of a book entitled *Practical Applications of Dynamic Symmetry*. One chapter is entitled "The Law of Phyllotaxis." A copy of pages 27 and 28 is attached hereto.[2] Mr. Hambidge demonstrates that Greek art is based on the summation series described above. My discoveries disclose the application of this Series in the following fields. Compare the numbers with the Summation series.

(3) The bodies of nearly all animals are composed of a torso and 5 projections therefrom: head and four legs. Birds have 5 projections from the torso: head, 2 wings and 2 legs.

(4) The human body is composed of a torso and 5 projections therefrom: head, arms and legs. The arms and legs are subdivided into 3 sections. The arms and legs end in 5 fingers or 5 toes. Each of these is again subdivided into 3 sections. There are 5 senses.

(5) Music. The best example is the piano. "Octave" means 8. In each octave there are 13 keys, composed of 8 white keys and 5 black keys. The black keys are divided into two groups, 2 and 3. A complete keyboard is composed of 89 keys.[3]

(6) Chemical Elements. There are approximately 89 primary elements.

(7) Human Activity. Ten years ago, I discovered that movements in the stock market, earnings and many other activities observed definite patterns continuously, in a "closed path in a diagram," and that each series "repeats itself" and does so in a "period of time," as shown in the definitions of the word "cycle." The results of my discoveries are disclosed in a Treatise entitled "The Wave Principle." The diagrams of patterns, wave numbers and periods of time follow precisely the Fibonacci Series. Subsequent to the publicationt of my Treatise, I learned of the discoveries of Mr. Hambidge and the Fibonacci Summation Series.

The sum of any two adjoining numbers of this series equals the next higher number, for example: 8 + 13 = 21.

The ratio of each number (above 5) to the next higher number is approximately .618. This ratio is present in many instances. For example, during the 13-year triangle of the stock market from November 1928 to April 1942, each wave of the triangle is .618 of its predecessor.

In his book, Mr. Hambidge says that this ratio fascinated the Greeks and he demonstrates how it dominated their art.

Dr. William F. Petersen, Professor of Pathology, University of Illinois, is the author of a very important and interesting book entitled *The Patient and the Weather*. Therein are graphs of the progress of a disease. The patterns of the record of the number of persons afflicted are precisely the same as any other activity, including the stock market, i.e., 5 waves upward.

(8) Time. The numbers of this Series are useful in the timing of waves, both advancing and declining. For example, the inflationary period from 1921 to 1929 consumed 8 years. Its correction, the triangle, from 1929 to 1942, consumed 13 years. Entire period of inflation and deflation, 21 years.

The Wave Principle is the application of Dynamic Symmetry to the stock market and all other human activities.

R.N. Elliott

FOOTNOTES

[1] Section (A) includes at least three periodicities which are "caused by various astronomical aspects." The first three might have been listed in this section. It is possible that Elliott is obliquely referring to the work of market predictors who use planetary alignments in their forecasting.

[2] See pages following Educational Bulletin X.

[3] Actually 88.

EDUCATIONAL BULLETIN Z
Nature's Law
May 3, 1944

Nature's Law is of practical value in all fields of human activity, and therefore important to everyone including business men, investors and young people. Its origin dates as far back as the Egyptian Pyramids, 3000 B.C. The basis and its application are demonstrated below.

The mathematical basis of Nature's Law is a summation series disclosed by Fibonacci, an Italian mathematician of the 13th century. This series follows:

1 - 2 - 3 - 5 - 8 - 13 - 21 - 34 - 55 - 89 - 144.

The sum of any two adjoining numbers equals the succeeding number, for example: 5 plus 8 equals 13. Any number, above 5, equals approximately 61.8% of the succeeding number. For example, 21 divided by 34 = 61.8%. Any number, above 5, divided by its immediate predecessor, equals approximately 1.618. For example, 34 divided by 21 = 1.618. This is called the reciprocal. Any number divided by its second predecessor equals 2.618, and so on.

The numbers should be memorized so that they may be recognized when they appear in the news, events, and in your own life. It is not nearly so difficult as the multiplication table. Everyone recalls that the clover has 3 leaves, but few know that it is one of the numbers of Nature's Law.

This summation series is the mathematical Law of Nature. By permission of Yale University Press, I include pages 27 and 28 from *Practical Applications of Dynamic Symmetry*, by Mr. Jay Hambidge.[1]

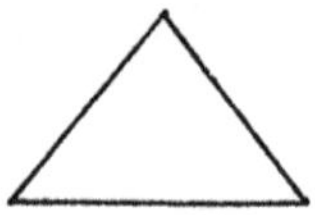

On his return to Italy from a visit to Greece and Egypt, Fibonacci disclosed the series. Pythagoras, a Greek philosopher, in 500 B.C. visited Egypt, and on his return he created this diagram. Thereunder, he placed the following cryptic inscription: "The Secret of the Universe." Presumably, it is intended to represent a pyramid. It will be noted that a pyramid is composed of 5 surfaces and 8 lines. The Great Pyramid is estimated to have measured originally as follows: base, 756 feet square, height, 481 feet. The ratio is 63.6.

The sunflower is only one of many demonstrations of Nature's Law. It is important to note that the maximum curve-crossing numbers are 89-144. The maximum number of practical use is $144,^2$ and very rare. 89 is more frequent.

When employing these numbers to time elapsed, if the number of days approaches 144, it is more practical to raise the unit of time to weeks. If the number of weeks approaches 144, it is preferable to increase the unit to months, then to years, decades or centuries. If all our months were arranged with 28 days each, or 4 weeks, there would be 13 months in a year.

The bodies of humans follow the numbers 3 and 5. From the torso there are 5 projections: head, 2 arms and 2 legs. Each leg and arm is subdivided into 3 sections. Legs and arms terminate in 5 toes and fingers. The toes and fingers (except the big toe) are subdivided into 3 sections. We have 5 senses. The monkey is the same as a human except that his feet are the same as his hands; that is, his big toe is the same as his thumb. Most animals have 5 projections from the torso: head and 4 legs. Birds have 5 projections from the torso: head, 2 feet and 2 wings.

Music: The best example is the piano keyboard. "Octave" means 8. Each octave is composed of 8 white keys and 5 black keys, total 13. A complete keyboard has 89 keys.

Chemical Elements: There are approximately 89 primary elements.

The Western Hemisphere is composed of 3 sub-divisions: North, Central and South America. In the Western Hemisphere, there are 21 republics, all of which are members of the Pan-American Union.

North America is composed of 3 countries, Canada, Mexico and the United States. South America is composed of 10 Republics and 3 European colonies, total 13. Central America was, previous to the Panama Canal, composed of 5 republics.

The United States was originally composed of 13 states. Today there are 55 sub-divisions as follows: 48 states, District of Columbia, Philippines, Panama Canal Zone, Puerto Rico, Alaska, Hawaiian Islands and the Virgin Islands.

On the Declaration of Independence, there are 56 signatures. The original number was 55. The last was added later.

Main branches of the Federal Government:	3	
Highest salute of the army:	21	guns
Voting age:	21	years
The Bill of Rights contains	13	points
Number of colors in the National flag:	3	

The cornerstone of the Washington Monument in Washington, D.C. was laid July 4, 1848.

Total cost, $1,300,000, 13.

Height of shaft, 500 feet,	05.
Height of capstone, 55 feet,	55.
Base of shaft, 55 feet square,	55.
Top rim of shaft, 34 feet,	34.
Steps of foundation, 8,	08.
Windows (2 on each side),	08.

The capstone is in the form of a pyramid. The base is 34 feet square, height is 55 feet, ratio is .618.[3]

The Axis is composed of 3 partners. Germany dominated 13 countries in rapid succession but stalled on the 14th, Russia. Mussolini served as dictator for 21 years.

In 1852, Commodore Perry paid a courtesy visit to Japan and invited the "Son of Heaven" to abandon absolute isolationism. In 1907, 55 years later, Japan seriously threatened the United States. In 1941, 34 years later, and 89 years from 1852, Japan attacked Pearl Harbor.[4]

Human activities move in waves employing all the numbers of the summation series. The principle movements are covered by the numbers 1, 3 and 5, but of several degrees, such as Minor, Intermediate and Major. A partial list of human activities follows:

Price of securities, such as individual stocks, bonds, groups and averages,
Volume of industrial production, both individual and national,
Movements of persons from cities to farm and vice versa,
Volume of securities traded,
Commodities,
Patents applied for,
Epidemics,
Price of Gold,

New Insurance,
Lend-Lease,
Temperature, etc., etc.

Waves form definite patterns. A bull movement is composed of 5 waves. Waves 1, 3 and 5 are upward, waves 2 and 4 downward or sidewise. A bear movement is composed of 3 waves.

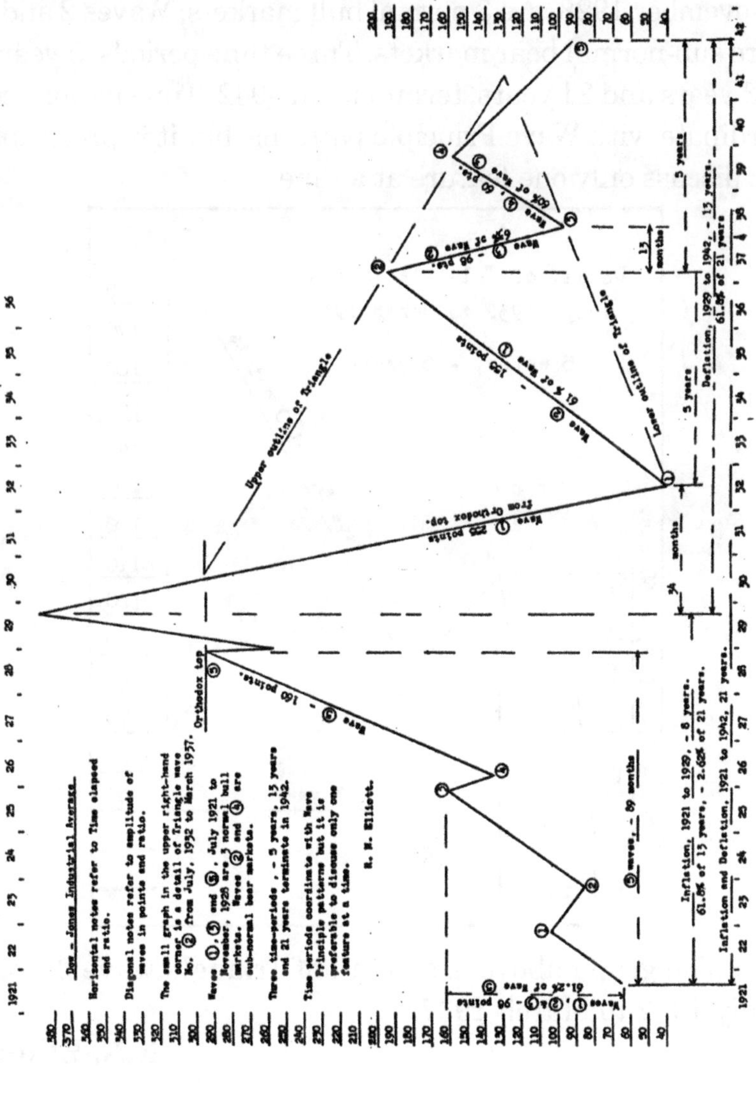

The accompanying graphs of the Dow Jones Industrial Average demonstrate the application of the numbers of the summation series in waves, amplitude of movements and time elapsed, by ratio.

In these diagrams, horizontal notes refer to time elapsed and ratio, while diagonal notes refer to amplitude of waves in points and ratio. Waves 1, 3 and 5, July 1921 to November 1928, are 3 normal bull markets. Waves 2 and 4 are sub-normal bear markets. Three time periods, 5 years, 13 years and 21 years, terminate in 1942. Time periods co-ordinate with Wave Principle patterns, but it is preferable to discuss only one feature at a time.

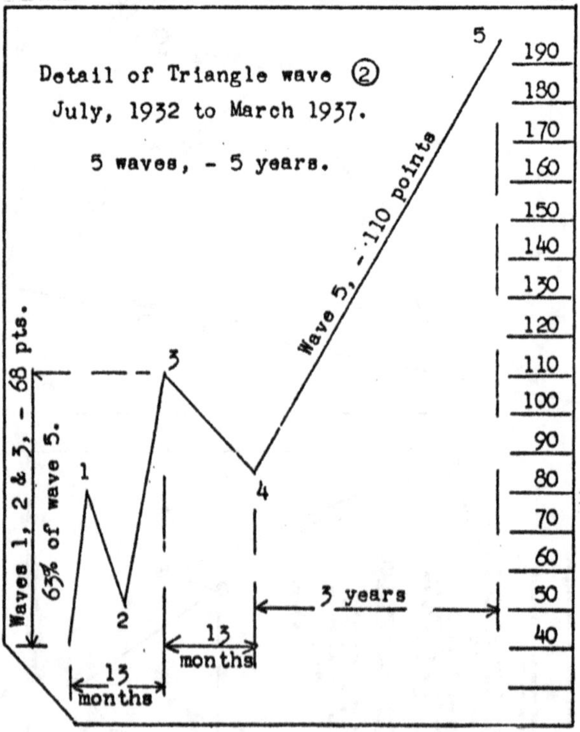

The graph above is a detail of Triangle wave 2 from July 1932 to March 1937.[5]

R.N. Elliott

FOOTNOTES

[1] See pages following Educational Bulletin X.

[2] He means both in nature and in analyzing phenomena that reflect the Wave Principle.

[3] Many of these measurements (assuming they are accurate) may well have been consciously included.

[4] Should the U.S. watch out for Japan in 1996?

[5] Legs of a triangle should be composed of three waves, according to Elliott's rules. As opposed to the convoluted reasoning referenced in Footnote 8 with Interpretive Letter No. 17, the count shown in this graph is the correct one, which Elliott apparently never fully abandoned.

EDUCATIONAL BULLETIN ZA

Alternation[1]

June 7, 1944

Alternation: "Occurrence or action of two things or series of things, in turn." Alternation is a Law of Nature.

Leaves or branches often appear first on one side of the main stem and then on the opposite side, alternating their position.

The composition of the human body follows the same rule:

1st: Projections from the torso, head, arms and legs, total 5.
2nd: Legs and arms are subdivided into 3 sections.
3rd: Legs and arms terminate in 5 toes or fingers.
4th: Toes and fingers are subdivided into 3 sections.

Thus: 5 - 3 - 5 - 3.

An endless list of examples could be cited, but the objective of this discussion is the habit of alternation in human activity.

Bull and bear markets alternate. A bull market is composed of 5 waves and a bear market of 3 waves. Thus, 5

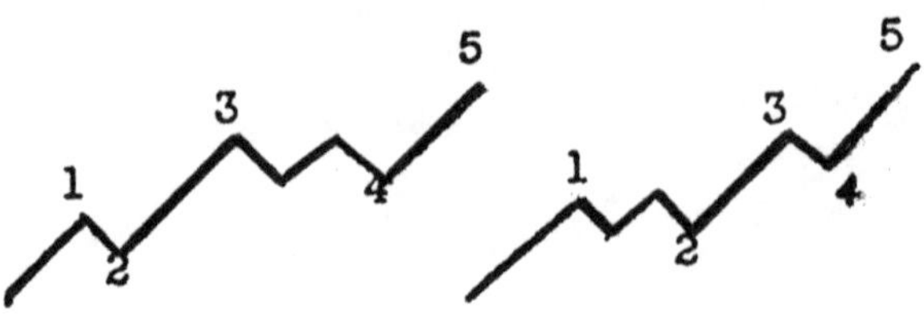

and 3 alternate. The same rule governs all degrees. A bull movement is composed of 5 waves. Waves 1, 3 and 5 are upward. Waves 2 and 4 are downward, or sidewise. Thus, the odd numbers alternate with even numbers.

Waves 2 and 4 are corrective. These two waves alternate in pattern. If wave 2 is "complex," wave 4 will be "simple," or vice versa. A "simple" correction in the smaller degrees is composed of one wave downward. The "complex" is composed of 3 waves, downward or sidewise. See preceding diagrams.

In the larger degrees, such as complete bull markets, the corrective waves of the bear market are correspondingly larger. These are shown in my Treatise on page 17, paragraph 1. Preparation for the final down swing is often tedious. First there is a downward movement of some importance which I letter with a capital "A." This is followed by an upward swing and is designated as wave "B." The third and last movement downward is wave "C." wave "A" may be a "zigzag" pattern. In this event, wave "B" will be a "flat," inverted. If wave "A" is a "flat," wave "B" will be a "zigzag," inverted.[2] In any event, wave "C" will be composed of 5 waves down. It may be severe and approach the starting point of the previous bull market, as per diagram "C," paragraph 1, page 17. Thus, waves "A" and "B" alternate. The 13-year triangle furnishes an example. From November 1928 to March 31, 1938 is a "flat."[3] From March 31, 1938 to October 1939 is a "zigzag" inverted. From October 1939 to May 1942 is a "flat."

An "irregular" top is one in which wave "B" exceeds the top of the 5th wave of the previous bull market, as explained in my Treatise. Even these alternate. The top of 1916 was "irregular." In 1919 the top was "regular." In 1929, the top was "irregular," and in 1937 "regular."[4]

Up to 1906, the Rails led upward movements. For 34 years, from 1906 to 1940, the Industrials led upward movements. Since 1940, the rails have been leading.[5] This was demonstrated in Interpretive Letter No. 29.

R.N. Elliott

FOOTNOTES

[1] This is an extremely important concept.

[2] This relationship, if it occurs at all, is not a common occurrence.

[3] See Footnote 7 of Interpretive Letter No. 17.

[4] There is no separate concept necessary in the Wave Principle with respect to irregular tops. If an orthodox top is followed by an irregular correction, wave B will naturally make a new high. Calling the 1916 and 1929 tops irregular, moreover, stretches the concept of a flat correction to include obviously non-flat structures. In his examples, 3-3-5 (irregular-zigzag-5) patterns are much better abandoned in favor of placing the orthodox top at the actual peak, with a simple zigzag thereafter.

[5] See Interpretive Letter 23, Footnote 3.

[From a circular on R. N. Elliott's services]

November 6, 1944

Market movements repeat in identical waves. These waves are uniform because they reflect a natural law, a law known, as far back as early Greece, a law that operates, not only in the stock market, but throughout the animate and inanimate world.

Thus, the broad pattern of one bull market conforms to the pattern of another; the broad pattern of one bear market, to the pattern of all other bear markets. Compare, for instance, the bull swing of the 'Twenties with the bull swing of the 'Thirties and observe the identical wave formation.

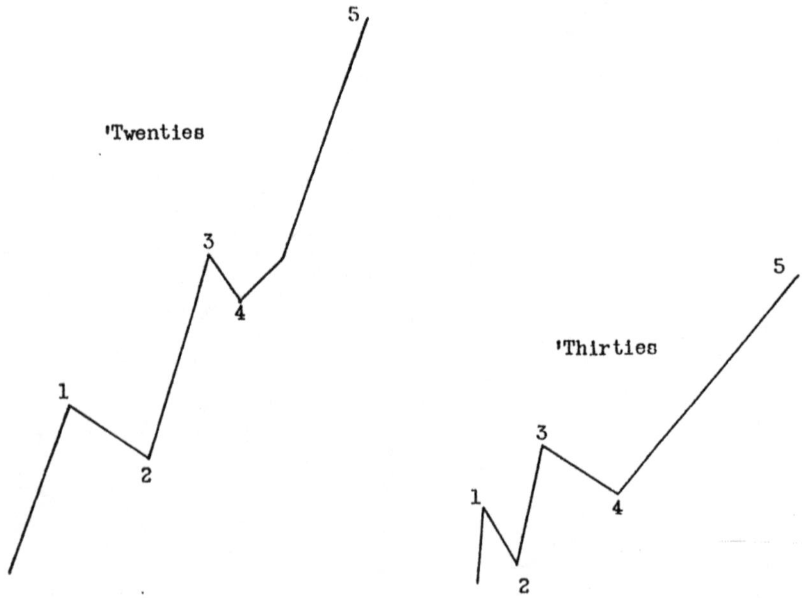

The Wave Principle is a Law of Nature, not a theory or gadget.

My Educational service completely acquaints the student of stock market phenomena with the laws of the wave movement, of which the above is a simple illustration. It is designed to so thoroughly train him in reading current trends and forecasting pending trends, minor, intermediate, and major in character. Thus, those who learn the valuable principles of this fundamental law need no longer rely on others for market advice but can read and project the market for themselves.

During the period that the wave movement is being taught, my forecasting service, working entirely with the law of the wave movement, accompanies the educational service. Thus, it offers market guidance during that period when the subscriber is in the process of learning wave movement phenomena, and it is likewise interpretative in character, thus further grounding the subscriber in the important principles under discussion. This forecasting service points out market trends and, at important turning points, gives specific stocks for purchase or sale.[1]

FOOTNOTES

[1] Elliott does not recommend specific stocks in any of the periodicals reprinted in this book. The Forecast Letters marked "Confidential," of which so few survive, may have included such recommendations.

Miracle of the Ages[1]

December 20, 1946

1. Exhaustive research of stock market cycles resulted in the publication of a Treatise in 1938. Subsequent discoveries resulted in the publication in June 1946, of a second Treatise entitled "Nature's Law." Numerous pages are dedicated to the Great Pyramid Gizeh, as I found that the symbols coincided with my discoveries.

2. I have read several books relative to this pyramid. Among them is one that a friend recently sent me entitled *Miracle of the Ages*, by Worth Smith (published and for sale by Elizabeth Towne Publishing Co., of Holyoke, Mass., price, $1.10 post paid).

3. The outstanding features of the pyramid are:
   a. Accurate long range predictions.
   b. Novel methods of recording predictions.
   c. Advanced mathematics.
   d. Knowledge of astronomy.
   e. Enormous expense of construction.
   f. Engineering ability of high order.
   g. Numerous citations in the Bible that coincide with forecasts in the Pyramid.[2]

4. The names of the architects are not known, but their origin and nationality are surmised.

5. The date of construction was approximately 46 centuries ago.

6. The birth of Jesus the Christ was predicted to the day, 2644 years before it occurred.[2]

7. Investigators of recent years learned how to decode the symbols of prediction, but not how to forecast. The elevation of the pyramid is given, but little is said concerning the outside pattern as described in "Nature's Law" on pages 7 to 10, 51, 56 and 57.

8. Pythagoras (500 B.C.) and Fibonacci (1300 A.D.) had no opportunity of learning anything concerning the symbols inside the pyramid. Their observations were therefore confined to outer symbols, such as the pattern of the pyramid and its elevation, 5,813 inches,[3] which is the secret of forecasting. See page 9, paragraph 3.

R.N. Elliott

P. S. Errata in "Nature's Law."[4]

Page 7, paragraph 4. "B C" should read "A D."

Page 14, Intermediate degree, wave 2. "AA C" should read "A B C."

FOOTNOTES

[1] See Footnote 1 of the "Confidential" Forecast Letter dated July 23, 1946.

[2] Elliott is accepting some rather dubious claims here.

[3] I.e., 5-8-13.

[4] These were corrected for *R.N. Elliott's Masterworks*.

Ratio Ruler
See instructions
on the facing page.

Applicable only on
arithmetic scale.

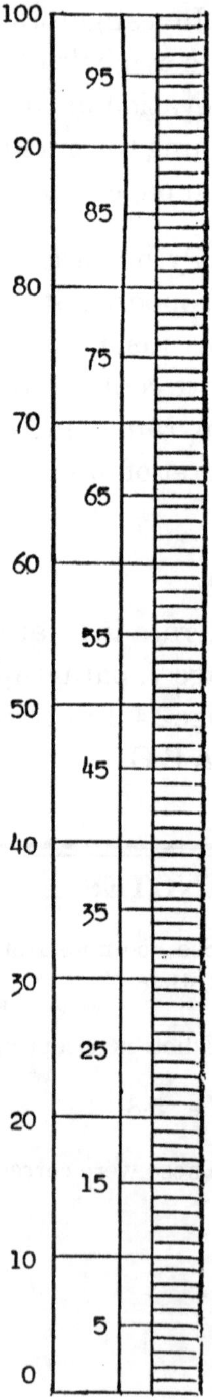

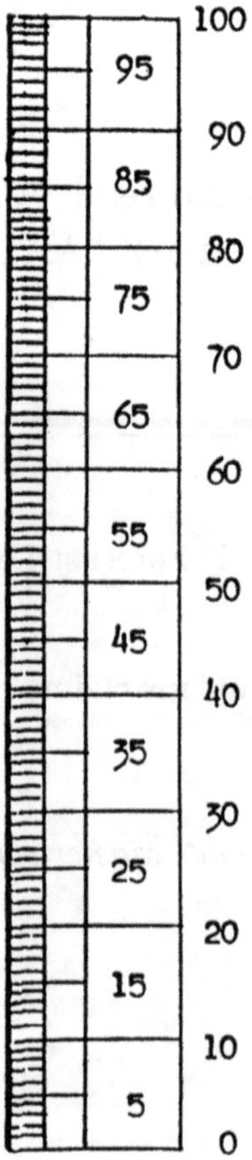

The distance from 0 to any number on the left hand scale is equivalent to 61.8% of the distance from 0 to the same number on the right hand scale.

For example:

0 to 40 of the left hand scale
is 61.8% of
0 to 40 of the right hand scale.

In reverse:

0 to 40 of the right hand scale is
equivalent to 1.618% of
0 to 40 of the left hand scale.

R.N. Elliott

THE WAVE PRINCIPLE

63 WALL STREET
NEW YORK 5, N.Y.

R. N. ELLIOTT

August 12, 1946

Mr. A. E. [redacted]
P. O. Box [redacted]
[redacted] New York

Dear Mr. [redacted]

Many thanks for your letter of August 7th. With reference to your request for previous Letters, - one of the several reasons why I published "Nature's Law" was the fact that the supply of many previous Letters was exhausted. Note on page 1 the following statement "All disclosures herein have been previously copyrighted". In the event that it may be of service to you I am sending by parcel post a copy of my 1938 Treatise and such Letters and Bulletins as can be spared. Some were issued before I had discovered and solved the 13 year triangle.. In "Nature's Law" note paragraph 4 page 18. Wave (5) of the 13 year triangle started 1939.

Being the discoverer of the phenomenon and the basis thereof I have spent much time coordinating the facts and finding historic background. Probably I have only scratched the surface. Even so some say that "Nature's Law" is the discovery of the age.

While my fee is small, as you say, some clients pay much more for special service. I have an inquiry for 400 copies of "Nature's Law".

I suggest that you read the book several times.

Being unable to comply with your request for all back Letters I return your check. Incidentally you will find a few (very few and unimportant) differences between the old and new Treatises, - notably in the use of arithmetic and semi-log scales. In 1938 I knew nothing about the background nor the 13-year triangle then in process. Much time was consumed working out the correlation on page 31.

At the moment I do not know what Letters I may be able to send you.

Yours very truly,

R. N. Elliott

RNE:PC

Excerpt from

New Methods For Profit in the Stock Market

by Garfield Drew (1955 edition)1

1954 REVIEW

Section V

Cycle Forecasting

After a brave start in 1949-1951, the past two years, at least, have detracted from the long-term 1948 forecasts of most basic cycles. There is one exception, however, that will be discussed later in detail.

The original 1948 text of this book said in the conclusion to the section on cycles that the studies analyzed implied a rising trend ahead for stock prices, despite the pessimistic mood of that era. But it also added that there was a somewhat similar agreement thereafter as to a serious decline that would reach bottom around 1952.

So, these cycles were only half right at the time. They were correct that an important upward trend lay ahead, but wrong in assuming that it would be over soon and be followed by a severe cyclical downswing that should theoretically have spent its force by this time.

It may also be instructive to compare the main conclusions of the book Cycles, as given on page 150, with the actual course of events. If these projections had been correct, stocks should have reached a bear market low in 1951, building activity should have been on the downgrade until 1953, and 1951-1952 should have been the trough of a depression.

As to the specific studies mentioned, no recent studies of the "Decennial Pattern" have appeared. The same is true of the Sidereal Radiation projections, which were accurate for a time, but, not surprisingly perhaps, failed to keep up the good record.

Marechal's long-term projection was not carried far beyond the point shown in the original discussion on pages 161-165. Consequently, there is nothing with which to compare performance in the current decade.

Elliott's Wave Principle (Pages 159-161)

This hypothesis seems to have stood up better than anything else in the field of long-range forecast. There was more hesitation of stock prices in 1947-1949 than originally anticipated, but the basic theory was quite correct that the next important move would not only be up, but also exceed the 1946 top.

At the same time, it was also forecast that, eventually, a fifth "wave" would exceed even the 1928-29 top for stock prices. That seemed utterly fantastic in 1948 when the 200 level would have looked "high," but with the Average having already hit 360 in 1954, it no longer appears quite so impossible of ultimate accomplishment.

Another interesting point that has emerged about the Wave Principle was its basically bullish position in 1953.2 When study of the "waves" comes down to the exact classification of the smaller intermediate movements, competent students can disagree. But in 1953, no matter how the smaller trends were classified, it all had to come out to the same thing in the end, namely, that the bull market had not ended in January 1953, and that the Industrial Average would reach a new high without any very serious intervening decline. Of course, this was borne out early in 1954 when the 300 level was reached for the first time in 24 years.

In 1954, the basic interpretation must still be that stock prices are in a large-size upside cycle that has nowhere near reached its apex.[3]

FOOTNOTES

[1] This book was originally published in 1948, the year Elliott died.

[2] This sentence refers to the analysis in A. Hamilton Bolton's first Elliott Wave supplement to his publication, The Bank Credit Analyst.

[3] All Elliott Wave supplements to the *Bank Credit Analyst*, as well as Hamilton Bolton's book, *The Elliott Wave Principle, A Critical Appraisal*, are available from New Classics Library (1993). These publications carry forward the practical application of the Wave Principle by Hamilton Bolton (with assistance from A.J. Frost, Charles Collins, Russell Hall and Walter White) up to 1970, with forecasts applicable through 1974. Robert Prechter's Elliott Wave reports began in 1976 and carry through to the present. Reprints of all issues are available.

"Elliott alone among cycle theorists (despite the fact he died in 1947, while others lived) provided a basic background of cycle theory compatible with what actually happened in the post-war period."

—A. Hamilton Bolton